Cruise America

A HISTORY OF THE AMERICAN CRUISE INDUSTRY

ROGER CARTWRIGHT & PETER RUSHTON

The
History
Press

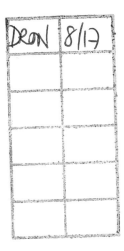
First published 2010

The History Press
The Mill, Brimscombe Port
Stroud, Gloucestershire, GL5 2QG
www.thehistorypress.co.uk

British Library Cataloguing in Publication Data.
A catalogue record for this book is available from the British Library.

ISBN 978 0 7524 4911 1

Typesetting and origination by The History Press
Printed in Great Britain
Manufacturing managed by Jellyfish Print Solutions Ltd

Contents

Note

In order to have a common denominator when discussing the size of ships, this book uses the measurement Gross Registered Tonnage (GRT). Tonnage is derived from the medieval word *tun*, or barrel. GRT is not a measure of weight but of capacity, representing the total enclosed volume of the ship in cubic feet divided by 100. Tonnage is the normal method of describing the size of a merchant vessel and is measured in accordance with the International Convention on Tonnage Measurement that came into force on 18 July 1982.

Whenever alterations are made to a ship her tonnage is subject to change, and careful scrutiny will sometimes reveal differences in the quoted tonnage of a vessel between one publication and another: unless significant, these are largely irrelevant, except to the dedicated ship enthusiast, and a general measurement of, say, 60,000 GRT should suffice to give the average reader an idea of a vessel's size.

In this book, when referring to the traditional liner trade (that is, the transportation of people from one place to another for any purpose other than casual vacationing), we have used the traditional term 'passenger'. In connection with cruising we have followed, wherever reasonable, the North American market terminology 'guest'.

Prinsendam at anchor.

Carnival Freedom displays her size and trademark winged smokestack at St Johns, Antigua.

About the Authors

Dr Roger I. Cartwright

International author and speaker, Dr Roger Cartwright, was born in Manchester, England, and worked as a teacher in the city before becoming a head teacher in Kent. In 1989 he switched careers and became a lecturer in the subject of management in higher education. He moved to Scotland in 1996 and retired in 2000 as the Director of the Centre for Customer Relations at Perth College – a constituent partner of the University of the Highlands and Islands. Roger is the author of twenty-six books on management, business, customer relations and teams and leadership. His work has been published in the UK, the USA, India, Greece and China. He is also the co-author of the first comprehensive study of the cruise industry. With Clive Harvey he wrote *Cruise Britannia*, about the British and cruising, published in 2004. They then wrote *The Saga Sisters*, a book dedicated to the ex-Norwegian America/Cunard liners *Vistafjord* and *Sagafjord* currently sailing as *Saga Ruby* and *Saga Rose*, a book that sold out the first edition in less than five months. His *P&O Princess: The Cruise Ships* was published in 2009 by The History Press.

In 2002, Roger was asked for his input into a Government report about possible mergers within the UK cruise industry involving P&O Cruises and Royal Caribbean. He has also worked in the UK, the USA and India. Roger spent a number of years as a consultant to a major air carrier, and has worked in New York, Boston, Los Angeles and Atlanta helping to train airline staff. He was attached to the Navy Days Organisation at Plymouth, and later Portsmouth, for eighteen years, with the rank of Lieutenant Commander Royal Naval Reserve. He is currently a life trustee of the Canadian Naval Memorial, the corvette HMCS *Sackville*, preserved in Halifax.

He has presented a series of maritime-themed talks on a number of cruise ships for both UK, other European, USA and Canadian passengers, and makes a point of matching the talks to the itinerary being followed.

Together with his wife June he lives in Crieff, Scotland, where they have a large collection of teddy bears. Roger is an avid railway modeller of both UK and USA prototypes. Roger also made a brief appearance in the feature film *Rocket Post* that won the Grand Prize at the 2004 Stonybrook Film Festival in New York.

Peter Rushton

Educated in Rhodesia, Peter ran away to sea as the 1950s drew to a close, joining the legendary Union-Castle Line as a deck cadet. He served his time on the African, Indian and Australian coasts, sailing in all manner of ships under the House Flag of the British & Commonwealth Group, Union-Castle's parent company. Qualifying as a deck officer he rejoined Union-Castle as junior fourth on their flagship *Windsor Castle*. He stayed on with the company for a time, before deciding to swallow the anchor and return to Rhodesia to seek his fortune ashore.

Joining the Government, he served as A.D.C to the last Governor of Rhodesia, Sir Humphrey Gibbs, in the period before Ian Smith's Declaration of Independence in 1965. After that event, Peter embarked on a new career in industry, but his love and abiding interest remained ships and the sea. The exploits of the great navigators fascinated him, and he nurtured his love of ships by reading countless books on the great liners that had sailed the seas a few short years before his day as a young merchant seaman.

Today, Peter devotes his working life to the cruise industry. He and his wife, Rosemary, specialise in arranging Lecture and Enrichment Programmes for many major cruise lines, and their company, the P&R Agency Ltd of Sussex, England, ranks high among the leaders in this specialised field.

Peter is a regular columnist for *World of Cruising* magazine and is a regular speaker on cruise ships, talking on both maritime and ocean liner history and the destinations being visited.

Introduction

The rising sun, quickly dissipating the cool of early morning, glints off the pristine white paintwork of the berthing cruise ship, her guests impatient for their shoreside venture. In the bay, the distant clatter of an anchor chain signals the arrival of yet another vessel, her population clamouring for the start of the tendering operation. A typical twenty-first-century morning that is being repeated, almost daily, right across the Caribbean Basin: the cruisers have arrived.

Compared with those of even fairly recent generations, these ships are huge, offering amenities undreamed of in their forbears: shopping malls, climbing walls, wave riders and ice rinks; theatres to rival the best on Broadway; restaurants and eateries to satisfy the most discerning gourmets; navigational equipment that would not have been amiss on an Apollo spacecraft. Many of their guests luxuriate in multi-level staterooms, and even the lowliest enjoy en-suite facilities. They have come from all points of the compass: Pittsburgh, New York, the Mid-West, California and Florida. Nearly every State in the Union is represented amongst the average 2,500 guest complements.

Fairly large contingents of Canadians mingle with their British counterparts, whilst smatterings of other nationalities – Mexicans, Argentinians, Germans, Dutch and French – all join the disembarkation lines, digital cameras poised, cellphones locking into new networks, all ready for the excitement of yet another new port. To join the ship in Miami they have flown on a number of different airlines transiting through Denver, Phoenix, Dallas, Newark and Chicago, and the truly multi-national crew comprising perhaps thirty different nationalities have come from much farther afield – from Europe, the Philippines, Thailand, Poland, or the Ukraine, there may even be a few Americans amongst the staff!

Whatever their origins, amongst the guests anticipation for another day in paradise is almost universal, although the reality might prove a little different. A small Caribbean island can see its population increase dramatically with the onslaught of seven or eight mega-ships, and the resultant jostling crowds can prove exhausting. Part of their first view of paradise will be the same sights that they saw on yesterday's island: Columbian Emeralds, Diamonds International, H. Stern and

others, as poised here today as they were yesterday, and as eager as they will be again tomorrow. The day ahead will be hectic, but still a great experience, much sought after by growing numbers of vacationers from all over the world, especially from North America.

Ocean liner purists are often given to describing the modern cruise ship as a floating condominium, and mocking her chunky lines and slab-sided proportions. In some respects their comments are justified. The cruise ship of today does not incorporate in her design the graceful sheer of old, or the cruiser-stern and finely flared bows. But, she is still a ship, with a beauty that is new and different, and she still has a soul. Others speak of her as a floating resort, and in many respects this is true, for her owners and designers have deliberately created her to be one. If enough amenities can be provided aboard, then the guests may prefer to spend their holiday dollars without setting foot ashore – and on-board revenue is the watchword.

At the other end of the scale, smaller and more intimate ships have been described as country clubs, and this too is a deliberate ploy on the part of shipowners, who believe that their market lies in the 'exclusive' domain. In short, there is literally something for everyone, and although many of the amenities are innovative, some are not, and many of the classic ocean liners of yesteryear featured attractions that are commonplace today.

For example, *Willhelm Gustloff* of 1938 boasted that the greater majority of her guest cabins were outside; *Arandora Star* of 1928 had outdoor swimming pools; the Italian liner *Rex*, Blue Riband holder of her day, sported a Lido Deck, and the *Queen Mary* and *Normandie* of the 1930s had dedicated shopping malls. Even the alternative dining, so avidly sought by today's cruisers, was available in the Ritz-Carlton Grill of the 1905 liner, *Amerika*.

In the past, of course, facilities like these were the preserve of the wealthy, and class distinction prevailed, whereas the facilities on today's ships are available to all guests. Public areas and cabins on modern ships are superb. Those who criticise the modern ship because of her outward appearance need to remember that it is what the guest sees on the inside that counts, for it is his dollar that, ultimately, keeps the ship afloat. To most guests, outside appearance has no relevance at all.

This book is about the North American cruise industry – one that has grown from 4.25 million US individuals taking a cruise in 1992, to over 11.25 million in 2007. In addition, the number of Canadians cruising has risen from 150,000 to some 300,000 over the same period, and although these form a separate group in their own right, in this book they are deemed generic to North America. (As a matter of interest, and by way of comparison, the second biggest market is the British, which over the same period has grown from 225,000 to over 1.1 million.) It is almost impossible to list every ship and company that has operated within the North American market, so our observations are limited to the major developments that have made the North American market what it is today.

Whilst cruising grew out of the liner trade and the transportation of people from A to B, today it is an increasingly important part of the leisure/vacation market. A famous photograph of 1961 shows Luxury Liner's Row in New York, with Britain's *Mauretania* and *Queen Elizabeth* alongside US-flagged *United States* (the fastest liner ever built), *America*, *Independence* and the Greek ship *Olympia*, all awaiting or discharging trans-Atlantic passengers. However, unbeknown to shipowners and passengers alike, Armageddon for the liner had long lain just a smudge on the horizon. It is true that its advent went unrecognised, even when it arrived alongside. In some quarters, even the threat that it presented was dismissed as being of little consequence.

At about the time that *Normandie* was making her maiden voyage, an English inventor, Frank Whittle, theorised that an aircraft utilising engines of his design, each producing 10,000lbs of thrust at an astonishing 55,000ft of altitude, would be capable of travelling at 1,320mph, revolutionising intercontinental travel. His predictions came a step closer to reality when, in 1941, the Gloster-Whittle made its first flight into the jet age. Whittle's invention, coupled to the advances in airframe design prompted by the necessities of war, led inexorably to the first jet passenger aircraft.

In the early 1950s, a little under 40 per cent of all trans-Atlantic passengers travelled by air, enduring the discomfort of the lumbering noisy Skymasters, Stratocruisers and Constellations of the day. Then Boeing launched its ubiquitous 707, and the fate of the liner was sealed, for by the early 1960s over 60 per cent of travellers were taking advantage of the 6-hour flight, and by the middle of the decade the great ships like *Queen Elizabeth* were forced into a situation where their massive overheads and huge crews were serving passengers who represented perhaps 10 per cent occupancy. The position was unsustainable, and ship after ship was withdrawn from liner service.

When the *France* was withdrawn from service in 1974, only Cunard's *Queen Elizabeth 2* was left to operate a seasonal trans-Atlantic service: it seemed that such days were gone for ever as the aircraft ruled supreme. And yet, in 2007, the shipping terminals were full of even larger ships, all now engaged in cruising. Even *France* survived into the twenty-first century as the cruise ship *Norway*. Other great ships were mothballed. Some of them would, in due time, be reborn as cruise

ships thanks to the vision and drive of men like Knut Kloster and Ted Arison, who together formed Norwegian Caribbean Lines and started the modern Florida-based cruise – ball rolling in 1966 with *Sunward*.

This book is about cruising: the taking of an ocean voyage for the pleasure of the voyage itself, and not simply as a means of travelling from A to B. It is also about the North American cruise market, which by a long way is the largest segment of the cruise industry. Of the total 2007 cruise market of over 16 million, US cruise vacationers represented over 70 per cent of the total. This book looks at those companies and ships that are dedicated to this particular market.

Americans and Canadians may well be found in small numbers on British, German and Italian ships as well as those of other nations, just as Britons and others often take cruises on North American market vessels. Given the dominance of the US market, it must be said that it is on the ships operating in this sector that the widest choices of cruise will be found. So, it is hardly surprising that anything between 6 and 10 per cent of guests on a North American market ship hail from either Canada or the UK. However, the UK has its own thriving cruise business. We owe the North American cruise industry a great debt.

Many a ship buff will denigrate the modern cruise ship, describing it as a mere floating resort – 'Horizontal Hilton' is a phrase sometimes heard – but supporters of this view forget that the modern cruise ship is not a liner, but a highly sophisticated vessel in its own right, designed with the needs of the modern cruise customer in view, and that if the niceties of traditional ship design fall by the wayside then that is a justifiable sacrifice. The cruise market is a highly differentiated one. There are ships that operate in a more traditional manner; there are small luxury ships; there are ships that operate as floating country clubs and there are the 'fun' ships. We are in no doubt that the ocean liner purists will not take kindly to much of this book.

We do not believe that just because a ship is old it is necessarily classic. Too many older ships now cruise long after their sell-by date, with many of them used to develop a new market, and whilst that is a good thing, eulogising about these ships simply because they are old seems, to us, to be rather backward looking. Today's sophisticated guest expects a degree of luxury that was previously only available to a select few. To give an example, in 1972 the P&O cruise ship *Orsova* (previously in the liner trade), offered first-class cabins with bunk beds and no toilet facilities. It is difficult to imagine a cruise guest today accepting anything less than full en-suite facilities.

For many years, even the venerated *Queen Elizabeth 2* had cabins with bunk beds, but as her die-hard adherents began to fade from the scene, Cunard sensibly withdrew the vessel in 2009 and sold her for use as a conference centre. The most famous UK cruise ship, P&O's *Canberra*, was withdrawn in 1997 to scenes of lamentation in Southampton, but the poor old girl was tired and worn out and she had to go, no longer fitting in with the company's modern image.

Just as the steam locomotive became obsolete after the Second World War, so the advent of jet air transportation led to the demise of the ocean liner, as we have already said. Old liners finding temporary employment in the burgeoning cruise industry were always going to be stop-gap fillers, and before long the purpose-built ship would replace the obsolescence of yesteryear. For those who wish to read about some of the great liners of the past, there is a wealth of literature. Bill Miller, Clive Harvey and David Williams have all eloquently documented the days when people used ships not as a vacation, but as the means to travel between continents.

For those wishing to know more about the truly amazing range of facilities to be found aboard today's generation of ships, the Berlitz *Guide to Cruising* and *Cruise Ships*, edited by Douglas Ward and published annually, is a superb reference work. Other texts are less useful, except to the true ship enthusiast, with many of them simply providing endless lists of ships and statistics. They are of little practical use, giving scant information about particular companies, their philosophies, markets or customers.

Although the majority of the photographs in this book are of ships, we hope that the reader will find that there is more substance to our narrative, for we are not trying to present a book of lists, rather we are trying to portray the enormous diversity of elements which contribute to the modern cruise experience – destinations, cuisine, entertainment, ambiance, service, shore excursions and imagination are all part of the package. Just a few short years ago, who would have thought of wave riders, climbing walls, skating rinks, central parks and grassy golf links aboard a ship. Here lies the nitty gritty: the ship is important, but it is not the only thing that attracts the fare payers!

In making their decision about which product best fits their desires, customers have considered:

> Guest demographics
> On-board currency
> The cuisine
> The entertainment

In a given cruise scenario, it is fair to assume that if most of the guests for the majority of the time on board are from the US or Canada; if the currency used on board is the US dollar; if the food on offer is typical of North America, and if the entertainment provided is in American English and targeted at a North American audience, then the product is aimed at the North American market.

So, let us examine why people take a cruise.

WHY DO PEOPLE CRUISE?

People take holidays for a variety of reasons. Some wish to simply relax, others want to explore or to socialise, to learn, to make new friends, and cruisers are no different. Their desires vary considerably according to age, lifestyle, previous experience, disposable income, available time and a miscellany of aspirations, but, at the end of the day, they are taking a holiday, and it is ultimately in this context that we have to consider them.

A sample of cruisers was asked to list their reasons for cruising. There were considerable differences found between the responses of those under and over fifty years of age:

	Under 50	Over 50
Culture	3	4
Entertainment	21	11
Children's Facilities	17	0
No/few children	1	9
Safety	12	31
Pampering	7	12
Special Occasion	12	0.5
Romance	0	0.5
Climate	15	6
Food	6	7.5
Ease of travel	5	12
Recuperation	0	0.5
Social	1	6
	100	100

Figure 1: Reasons for Cruising

Climate was more important to the under fifties, as were entertainment and facilities for children (very important to the under-thirty-five age group and an area of significant potential growth for the industry). The ranking for climate (third overall in the under fifties group), may seem surprising, especially as some of the newer cruising areas like Alaska, Iceland, Cape Horn, Norway and around Britain are not renowned for warm, sunny, days.

In general terms, the sample showed that the main factors in favour of cruising against other forms of vacation fell into three main categories:

Carnival Pride at anchor.

Crown Princess of 1990 became the German market *Arosa Blu* and then *Ocean Village 2*.

As *Crown Princess*, *Ocean Village 2* had revolutionary lines when introduced in 1990.

Many US market ships have a jogging track – like Seven Seas' *Mariner*.

Relaxation

The popular perception of the cruise being a place to lie in the sun whilst enjoying the benefits of wafting sea breezes is certainly one element placing relaxation at the top of the scale, but it is by no means the only one. The convenience of arriving at the ship, unpacking only once and then having your hotel room move with you from place to place is another, and the fact that entertainments are close at hand and inclusive, a third.

Safety

Cruising was seen as a safe method of seeing the world, with older people especially appreciating the fact that they could enjoy evening entertainment without having to take any risks: the self-contained aspect of cruising was especially important to them.

Social

Cruising was seen to be more exclusive than other package vacations, a perception that is both a strength and a weakness. Confirmed cruisers appreciate the exclusivity in both the type of fellow cruisers and the social cachet of being a guest, whereas exclusivity was quoted as a major factor for not taking a cruise package by non-cruisers, the latter holding a widespread belief that the atmosphere might be too stuffy, with insufficient activities in the, perceived, confined spaces of a ship.

Reasons for Not Cruising

It is as important to consider why 98 per cent of the population have never taken a cruise, compared to the estimated 2 per cent that have. Discussions with people who had not considered cruising, or had rejected the concept, revealed five main reasons, all of which co-related to the findings of other studies:

Expense

Cruising was seen, rightly, as being at the expensive end of any holiday price range. There was no general awareness of the range of prices on offer, and when asked to estimate the cheapest cruise, the majority of those questioned over-estimated the minimum cost of a cruise by nearly 100 per cent. In recessionary times, with high unemployment figures, it is understandable that people are reluctant to spend the perceived large amount necessary for a cruise, yet within the North American cruise market there has been considerable discounting which has widened, dramatically, the scope for the would-be first-timer. This, in turn, has led to a greater emphasis on on-board revenue generation, and retail activities such as art auctions have become a major part of many American market cruise operations. Another major revenue generator is the on-board casino.

Exclusivity

Cruising was often seen as being socially exclusive, with many holding the view that it was only for the wealthy. The idea of taking a cruise appears to be one use for large-scale lottery winnings. It is clear that the cruise companies still have some way to go to ensure that holidaymakers are made aware of the fact that cruising can (and does) cater for a wide variety of market segments. More and more ships pander to middle-income families, and the cost of a cruise compared to the rise in personal income in the developed world appears to have declined, making it a more affordable vacation option.

Family

Cruising is still seen by many as a vacation for couples and not suitable for children. The newer entrants to the market and many of the latest ships from traditional cruise companies have excellent facilities for children. The fact that Disney has entered the cruise market provides evidence of a significant market initiative geared towards the family. The major mainstream American market cruise companies, Carnival, Royal Caribbean and Norwegian Cruise Line, all have superb packages for infants, children and teenagers, making their products very family friendly.

Claustrophobia

There was little appreciation of the size of modern cruise ships amongst those who had not taken a cruise. Claustrophobia was mentioned frequently, but when asked to conceptualise the space on board a 100,000+ GRT-ship, the awareness was lacking. People believed that there would be no quiet spaces.

Not all Alaskan cruise ships are huge
– Cruise West's *Spirit of '98*.

Little and large – *Amsterdam* alongside *Ocean Majesty* at Tallin.

A sign of the times, a Mexican patrol boat protects American market cruise-ship passengers.

Seasickness

Often quoted, seasickness appeared to be a major factor in not taking a cruise. Modern stabilised ships and new drugs significantly reduce the effects of this ancient malaise (of which Nelson was a frequent sufferer), but the fear of discomfort appeared to be very marked.

As a part of the wider world of tourism, cruising depends on other sectors of the industry for its growth and development, especially air transport and resort hotels. These linkages have been exploited very successfully with American market cruise companies (as will be shown in the case study later relating to the Princess operation in Alaska), but it is a truism that, whilst jet air transportation killed off the traditional liner trade, it has today contributed to the rise in cruising, allowing companies to operate cruises from base ports far removed from North America.

The Cost of Cruising

In 1997, when Dickinson and Vladimir wrote *Selling the Sea*, the issue of discounting was already contentious. Whilst supermarkets may offer 'loss leaders' to entice customers into the store, cruise companies often appear to do the opposite. The initial brochure price may well be much higher than the discounted price available to the guest. If the brochure price for a particular stateroom on a particular cruise is $3,000 per person, then a discounted price of $1,800 appears to be a bargain. The fact is that, having seen a price of $3,000, the guest will want a cruise perceived to be worth $3,000, and not one worth $1,800. How can cruise operators deliver and still generate enough revenue to cover costs and make a reasonable profit?

In times of recession or national emergency (such as 9/11), a cruise company may decide to operate at a loss in order to maintain its customer base and meet cruise schedules. Obviously such a strategy is not sustainable over anything but the short term. In more normal economic times, the laws of supply and demand operate. The earlier a cruise is booked, the greater the discount. The company has what it hopes is a confirmed booking, and on the basis that 'a bird in the hand is worth two in the bush', is prepared to make less profit in return for certainty.

In economic parlance, a cruise is deemed to be a perishable good, for once the ship has sailed an empty cabin remains just that. Therefore, as sailing date approaches, vacant cabins may be sold at a large discount. As long as the costs of the guest being on board (food, port taxes etc.) are covered, then any extra revenue generated will contribute to profits. In the current climate it seems that all cruises are being discounted, which inevitably begs the question as to whether the brochure price is merely a hook upon which to hang the appeal of the bargain.

However, the guest should be aware that the company will seek to make up for the discount through on-board revenue generation. The less expensive or the more discounted the cruise, the more likely the guest is to be bombarded by on-board revenue opportunities. Art auctions, photographs taken by the holder of the line's photographic franchise, drinks promotions, alternative extra-cost restaurants, shore excursions and the like, are just some of the major on-board revenue generators which can add significantly to the price of a cruise, and can provide a nasty surprise at the end of the cruise when the final account is rendered.

As the recession of recent years began to bite, there were more and more special offers, including two-for-one deals and free air travel, all designed to entice new, as well as existing, customers. In general, the price of cruising within the North American market has been falling relative to salary levels. Increased competition has driven down prices considerably, bringing more and more potential customers into the industry. However, costs have also risen, particularly the price of oil, so that cruise operators face a delicate balancing act to ensure that costs are covered and profitability maintained.

Tipping

The origin of the word tips lies in the phrase **T**o **I**nsure **P**ersonal **S**ervice. Logically, that suggests that tips should be given at the beginning of a cruise and not at the end. It would be unacceptable in this day and age to expect cruise passengers to have to pay upfront for good service, although many lines suggest just that. Tips can be pre-paid, although what happens in the case of bad service is problematic – a visit to reception to have them removed may end up confrontational.

Tips were traditionally given on the final night/morning of a cruise, with recipients being the stateroom steward or stewardess and the dining room servers, the people who have the most contact with the individual cruise guest. However, the provision of good cabin and table service requires the input of people whom the guest may never meet – laundry staff, washing-up staff, cooks and the like –

who would receive nothing in terms of tips unless companies operated a policy of pooling tips or, as actually happens, the backroom people are tipped, in turn, by those at the coal face.

The advent of alternative dining options means that one may be served by many different people when eating – which presents the dilemma, who deserves the tip? Many companies now add tips to the final account for the 'convenience of guests', and then allow the guest to alter the amount as required. Many of the more upmarket cruise lines, such as Regent Seven Seas and Silversea, actually include tips within the price.

The Environmental Bubble

There are plenty of Italian, Spanish and British cruise ships operating in the Mediterranean, so why do the majority of Americans not book a cruise on one of them? For the same reason that most British cruise passengers book on a British, rather than an American, market ship in the Caribbean. Generally, people like to be surrounded by that which is familiar for at least part of their vacation.

An American market ship operating between Sydney and Auckland, and thus remaining within an English-speaking area, is nevertheless a slice of America. The customs, food and entertainment cater to American tastes, and would not be the same on, say, a British ship operating the same route. American bacon is different to Canadian bacon and different again from British bacon. Eggs are prepared differently in the UK to America. Jokes by comedians do not always travel well. Folk like what they know, and often know what they like! In effect, the cruise companies are offering their customers a true home from home, and cruising allows the customer to experience foreign travel from the comfort zone of a familiar environment.

The North American market product has, traditionally, been more destination intensive than that of the UK, the next biggest sector. There are as few days at sea as possible, and the cruise calls at the maximum number of ports. In many ways this was a function of geography. Unless UK passengers are prepared to fly, there will be at least four days at sea just getting out to, and back from, the Mediterranean or Canary Islands sunshine.

Entertainment on North American market ships became more lavish, with professional performers being booked for solo performances, and professional dancers and singers being contracted to provide production shows that were less elaborate versions of those provided in resorts such as Las Vegas and Atlantic City. A common feature of Las Vegas and Atlantic City are the gambling facilities, known to be the principal magnets for the attraction of countless visitors. With this in mind, and conscious of the fact that, in the US, permission for the operation of casinos or other gambling operations is dependent on state law rather than federal law, cruise companies operating for the North American market identified early on that the provision of on-board gambling facilities would be a major generator of revenue, and began to allocate more and more space to their on-board casinos.

Designed for casino operations, this psychedelic gambling cruise boat was seen at Jacksonville, FL.

In recent years, a new form of revenue generation, the on-board art auction, has become popular, and is now to be found on many ships.

Class Distinction

Many North American cruise passengers spoken to by the authors have expressed their distaste for the traditional two-class ocean liner system. Modern cruise ships are one-class – or are they? More and more vessels provide enhanced facilities for those in premium-grade cabins and suites. Dedicated check-in, baggage handling and priority in booking alternative speciality restaurants are often the preserve of those who have paid the highest prices. A recent trend has been for the provision of special lounges for such passengers, a facility well-established on the QE2 with the Queen's Grill and its associated lounge for those in the most expensive accommodation. Is this the beginning of a return to the class system, or just normal differentiation? Cunard appears to be the main company operating such a system, although Holland America also has special facilities for its premium guests.

Market Differentiation

As previously mentioned, there are different national cruise markets – US & Canada, UK, Germany, Spain, France, Italy, Japan and Australia, to name a few. Many of the vessels operating in these national sectors began life in the American cruise market,

Queen Mary 2 –
classic livery,
stunning ship.

QE2 at Southampton.

Island Escape was better known in the US market as *Stardancer* and *Viking Serenade*.

Finally, we come to entertainment. Singers, instrumentalists, jugglers and magicians seem to be truly international, and one finds British, Australian and other English-speaking singers on board many American market vessels, alongside their US and Canadian colleagues. The same is true of the other types of acts. However, comedy does not seem to travel so well. There are comedians who can bridge the cultural differences, but in the main it seems that the US and the UK particularly are divided by a common language, and a comedian from the US and Canada who has been very successful in the North American cruise market may be less well appreciated on a British ship. Similarly, success with a British cruise audience is absolutely no guarantee that North Americans will respond in the same way.

Although it is becoming rarer for cruise ships to have headline stars on board (perhaps due to costs), the standards of entertainment remain high. American audiences are amongst the most demanding in the world, and will not tolerate low standards of entertainment.

Another area of differentiation relates to the length of cruise. European vacations are often taken in longer time periods than those in the US, with the result that in the US, 7-day cruises are common, whereas UK cruises are often 10–17 days in length, reflecting different vacation patterns.

A comparison of the 2010–2011 cruises offered by North American market cruise company, Princess Cruises, and the UK's Fred Olsen Cruise Lines, is shown below:

Duration	Princess	Fred Olsen
Less than 5 days	2%	7%
6–8 days	61%	19%
9–15 days	28%	60%
16 or more days	9%	24%

Figure 2: Comparison of Cruise Duration

Thus, whilst a major North American cruise company has 63 per cent of its cruises lasting less than 9 days, a British company catering for a similar demographic has 84 per cent of its offerings being of 9 days or more duration, the vast majority being actually in the 12–16 day bracket.

although there are exceptions. *Oriana* and *Aurora* of P&O, the German Aida ships, the fleet of the Mediterranean Shipping Company (MSC), a number of the Star Cruises vessels and the latest ships of Costa Cruises were designed and built specifically for their national markets. The differences are not great, but, notably, ships designed for the European market often have smaller casinos than those for the North American.

Research by the designers of *Oriana*, the first purpose-built cruise ship for the UK market – as late as 1995 – found that UK cruise passengers preferred smaller public rooms and more of them than American market passengers. They also found that it was necessary to fit more staterooms with bath tubs, as UK customers often prefer baths to showers. Entertainment venues on board have tended to be more lavish on American ships, although other sectors are catching up fast.

The provision of alternate dining venues has also been led by the American market, and this too is a feature to be found on the majority of new vessels in other areas. National tastes in cuisine are all important. Pizza parlours and burger bars are a notable feature of North American ships, and a company called American Family Cruises (an operation that never really made it off the ground), planned ISYSWASFIC parlours (I Scream, You Scream, We All Scream for Ice Cream) on its ships, but failed. As might be expected, food served in the restaurants usually reflects market tastes. There are those from outside the US and Canada who enjoy cruising on US market ships purely because the dining and entertainment experiences are different from those at home. At this point, one of the authors should state that in his experience the hamburgers served in the Waves Grill on board the Oceania ships are the best he has ever tasted anywhere!

Where do They Go?

North American guests cruise all over the world. In the 1990s, the Caribbean was the destination for around 66 per cent of them, according to research by Roger Cartwright and Carolyn Baird for their book *The Development and Growth of the Cruise Industry*, but this has changed as the market has grown. Research for this book, conducted via interviews, company information and published itineraries, shows that for 2010 the percentages of North Americans taking a cruise in particular areas are:

Norwegian Majesty under way.

Carnival Freedom displays her size and trademark winged smokestack at St Johns, Antigua.

REGION	%
CARIBBEAN	44
EUROPE	27
ALASKA	4
MEXICO/CENTRAL AMERICA	12
AUSTRALASIA	3
TRANS-ATLANTIC	3
SOUTH AMERICA	2
CANADA/NEW ENGLAND	2
MIDDLE EAST	1
ASIA	1
OTHER	1

Figure 3: Distribution of North American Market Destinations

Whilst the percentage cruising to the Caribbean is down sharply, it must be borne in mind that the North American (US–Canadian) market in 1999 was 5.75 million according to the Maritime Evaluations Group figures in the Berlitz *Guide to Cruising and Cruise Ships*. By 2009, this figure had more than doubled to nearly 12 million. Thus, if 66 per cent of 1999 North American cruise guests went to the Caribbean, this would equate to 3.8 million visitors. In 2010, the 44 per cent quoted above provides 5.3 million.

That the Caribbean Islands can absorb 3.8 million cruise guest visits per year (excluding those from UK, Italian, German, French etc.) is amazing, but to absorb 5.3 million is perhaps stretching the infrastructure too much. Many of the ports in the Caribbean are extremely crowded, and the growth of huge shopping complexes has not added to the charm of the region. It is not the role of this book to discuss the economic, political and environmental issues relating to the cruise industry, but there are major issues caused by such huge flows of very transient visitors which must be addressed.

Europe has grown considerably as a North American cruise destination. Ease of flights and the ability of its major port cities to accommodate growing numbers of ships, coupled with its inherent cultural and historical interest, has made it a rapidly growing destination. By 2010, the major North American cruise companies were not only advertising directly to European markets (Royal Caribbean marketed heavily to the UK), but were positioning more and more vessels in Europe. In 2010, six Holland America vessels were relocated to Europe for extended seasons, following a successful move in 2009 by sister-brand, Princess, which relocated six.

In the future, we can expect to see the Middle and Far East regions becoming more and more popular, especially with more experienced cruise guests seeking new areas to explore. Naturally, political stability and safety are important, and as areas become safer, so the cruise ships follow.

Within any particular national market there is further differentiation. If somebody says ,'We are taking a cruise', it does not convey much information, as there are many types of cruise offered within the North American market. One really needs to ask, ' What type of cruise?'

Oceania's *Nautica* at
Darling Harbour, Sydney.

Star Princess
in Alaska.

Island Adventure in the
short cruise market out
of Port Everglades.

Navigator of the Seas
at Istanbul.

Amsterdam
at Istanbul.

The sleek lines of *Jewel of the Seas* at St Thomas.

Royal Caribbean's *Rhapsody of the Seas* alongside at Sydney.

Silver Cloud at Manaus on the Amazon, moored next to Cunard's *Caronia*.

Mariner of the Seas tenders at Cabo San Lucas.

CHAPTER ONE

Cruise America — A Brief History

THE EARLY YEARS

Cruising – as defined in the introduction, and as distinct from ocean voyages designed to transport an individual from one place to another (the liner or ferry trade) – made a fairly early entry into the shipping world after the advent of steam. Following numerous experiments in the UK, the USA and France, the first practical steam-driven vessel, the tug *Charlotte Dundas*, went into service on the Forth–Clyde Canal in Scotland in 1801. She was followed in 1807 by Foulton's New York-built *Cleremont*. Interestingly, the Royal Navy was loathe to give up its sail heritage, and whilst the USA completed a steam warship, the *Demologos*, just too late for the 1812 war with Britain, it was not until 1822 that the Royal Navy acquired a steamer in the form of the paddle-driven *Comet*.

Early steam ships used simple beam engines to drive paddles, the screw propeller not coming into vogue until 1844 with the launch of the USS *Princeton*. These early steamers were wooden vessels, and they only carried enough fuel for short coastal voyages. In January 1818, the Black Ball Line began the first scheduled passenger sailing across the Atlantic: using sailing ships, this was the first line to attempt to run to a timetable. In May of the following year, 1819, the fate of the sailing ship was sealed when the *Savannah*, under steam and sail, made the first steam-assisted crossing of the North Atlantic, taking nearly 28 days to make the crossing. The engines were used for only 80 hours of the passage.

Atlantic crossings by steam-powered ships, and voyages to South Africa and India, had become more frequent by 1839, when the British Admiralty awarded the UK–North America mail contract to a Canadian, Samuel Cunard. On 4 July of that year, in honour of the USA, Cunard's *Britannia* sailed from Liverpool and arrived at Halifax, Nova Scotia, on 17 July and Boston, Massachusetts, on the 20th. Ships such as the *Britannia* and Brunel's earlier *Great Western* (1838) made the North Atlantic crossing much safer for passengers than it was in the days of sail alone, and steam slashed passage times.

When Isambard Kingdom Brunel launched the *Great Britain* (3,270 GRT) in 1843, the world's first iron-hulled, propeller-driven passenger vessel set the pattern for future developments. *Great Britain* was rescued from her role as a hulk in the Falkland Islands in 1970, and is now superbly restored in Bristol, England, her birthplace. Sail was finally dispensed with as beam engines gave way to reciprocating ones, and then to turbines. Ocean voyages were now faster and considerably safer than they had been in the past, and a voyage could be taken for pleasure. Hitherto, and even in the early days of steam, there was nothing pleasurable about an ocean crossing: in the 1850s Dickens wrote of his cabin on *Britannia*, 'I have seen a smaller room but it was actually a coffin!' However, it was not long before ships became larger and facilities better.

In present-day terms, the first pleasure cruise was in 1881 when the Oceanic Yachting Company bought P&O's *Ceylon* and refitted her as a full-time cruise ship for the European market. By the early 1900s, White Star Line, P&O in their own right and the Hamburg America Line were offering regular cruises, and from the late 1890s the Orient Line were offering regular Caribbean, Mediterranean and Scandinavian cruises on board three of its vessels.

In 1900, Albert Ballin, Managing Director of the Hamburg America Line, introduced his company's first ever dedicated cruise ship, *Prinzessin Victoria Louise*. Modelled on the royal yachts of Europe, she offered an unprecedented all-suite accommodation to a wealthy and exclusive clientele. Sadly, she was wrecked after only six years in service, but her success prompted the conversion, in 1911, of the 16,502 GRT-liner, *Deutschland*, into the cruise ship *Victoria Luis*. She survived the war, but never returned to cruising, being converted to an immigrant ship. She was finally broken up in 1925. In 1912, Cunard introduced the first *Laconia* and the *Franconia* (traditional Cunard names), as their first dual-purpose cruise ships/liners. At this stage, cruising was still very much an ancillary affair to the main business of regular line voyages, and was an expensive vacation, open only to a privileged few.

Between 1912 and the outbreak of war in Europe in 1914, the British Royal Mail Company operated the small cruise ships, *Solent* and *Berbice*, on 7- or

14-day Caribbean cruises. The passengers joined the ship via the UK or New York to the Caribbean service, and returned home the same way – a precursor of today's fly cruising?

Following the end of the First World War, the shipping companies had a major shortage of tonnage for their core liner business, and even vessels taken in reparations from Germany were insufficient to meet the increased demand of traffic, especially on the North Atlantic. Emigration from Europe to North America resumed after the war, and the geopolitical changes to borders after the peace settlement of Versailles in 1919 caused major population displacements, especially in Eastern Europe. The United States received many of the displaced refugees, most of them through Ellis Island in New York Harbour.

Between 1892 and 1924, over 12 million immigrants arrived in New York alone. The vast majority of the liners then in service were unsuitable for pleasure voyages due to their design. They were, with the exception of the most expensive accommodation and first-class public rooms, utilitarian. Their *raison d'etre* was the efficient and economical transport of large numbers of people.

Orient Line in the UK resumed cruising in 1922, but it was in the US that the major expansion of cruising occurred, and this came about because of a bizarre political decision that is perhaps better known for the rise of gangsters such as Al Capone – Prohibition.

Booze Cruises

At midnight on 16 January 1920, the 18th Amendment to the Constitution of the United States prohibiting 'the manufacture, sale or transportation of intoxicating liquors', came into force. This measure had been under discussion for some time in an attempt to combat a belief that alcoholic consumption was affecting the moral and economic well-being of the USA. In 1870, there were 100,000 saloons in the USA, one for every 400 citizens. Only wines prepared for personal use in homes were exempted. All of a sudden, America could not drink.

Gangsters soon developed ways to process and supply alcohol, and the Federal Bureau of Investigation was tasked to prevent the trade – an impossible job, but for many law-abiding Americans, illicit drinking was not the answer. Ship-owners soon saw that there was a market gap they could meet. Whilst US-flagged vessels were unable to serve alcohol, once out of US territorial limits there were no restrictions on the ships of other flags.

Hamburg America, who had been operating *Resolute* and *Reliance* under the US flag, soon transferred their registry to Panama in order to capitalise on the opportunity, making a profit from the sale of alcohol once outside US territorial waters. This began the move to the 'flags of convenience' that still exist to this day. Many of the cruises out of US ports went nowhere. The ship would sail out on Friday night and return on Sunday, with its customers happy but hung-over. Some cruises would make for Halifax or Bermuda, but the aim of the passenger was simply to drink legally, rather than visit foreign destinations.

Luxurious accommodation, ornate public rooms, cuisine and entertainment, all so important today, were secondary to the opportunity to drink without fear of arrest or harassment. Prohibition registered cruising on the consciousness of the vacationing public, still a small minority, as an acceptable and fun way of enjoying an annual, or even a weekend, get-away.

The New York–South America service, operated by the British company Lamport & Holt, was a popular winter vacation run for those who could afford it, taking passengers away from the rain and cold and into the sun. As their ships, the *Vestris*, *Vauban*, *Vandyck* and *Vasari*, were UK registered, there was alcohol for sale as well! Unfortunately, the loss of the outbound *Vestris* in a collision off New York on 10 November, 1928, coupled with the Wall Street Crash of the next year, led to the company abandoning its New York passenger services.

Prohibition lasted until 1933, and cruises out of US ports provided a good way for shipping companies to gain a few more years out of tonnage that might otherwise have been sent to the breakers yard, as the new luxury liners of the 1930s with their better facilities, windows with sea views and art deco designs came into service. Ships such as the record-breaking *Mauritania* of Cunard spent their last few years cruising, and that company's *Berengaria* became known as the 'Bargain Area' in New York, so cheap were the passage prices, the company making its money instead on drink sales. A similar situation exists in some instances today, where low initial vacation prices are recouped through the on-board revenue-generation activities that have already been discussed.

On the North Atlantic, harsh winters led to an imbalance in passenger loads. Shipping companies needed enough vessels to cope with the spring and summer trade, but during the winter much of the tonnage would be laid up, earning no revenue, unless alternative employment could be found. The *Paris* of the French Line undertook cruises during her lay-off periods with a mere 300 guests, instead of her full capacity of 1,930. Many Cunard vessels were re-deployed, running cruises for the US market.

The *Laconia* (to be sunk during the Second World War with the loss of over 2,500 lives) undertook the first luxury world cruise as early as 1922, with the voyage taking twenty-two weeks. Later voyages boasted that Noel Coward was one of the passengers! In 1924, the *Belgenland* of Red Star Line undertook a 160-day world cruise with only 200 guests paying a minimum of $1,500 each – a considerable sum in 1924. She called at thirty-eight ports and managed to make a profit. Unfortunately, such high-end luxury cruises were badly hit by the Depression precipitated by the Wall Street Crash of October 1929.

Cabotage and Flags of Convenience

Cabotage is the transport of goods or passengers between two points in the same country. Originally only concerned with sea transportation, the term is now used to cover air, road and rail.

In the US, cabotage has been strictly applied to sea-borne trade between US ports through the provisions of the Merchant Marine Act of 1920 (commonly referred to as the Jones Act as it was sponsored by Senator W.L. Jones). The Act was designed to protect the US Merchant Marine as a strategic asset, although it has come under fire as being anti-competition. It does, however, provide crews of US-flagged vessels a degree of protection far higher than that of other countries.

The cabotage provisions of the Jones Act restrict the carriage of goods or, in the context of this book, passengers, between US ports to US-built and flagged vessels. In addition, at least 75 per cent of the crew members must be US citizens. There are also restrictive provisions covering the repair of US-flagged vessels by foreign shipyards. As far as the cruise industry is concerned, foreign-flagged vessels cannot embark guests in one US port and then proceed directly to another US port – they must visit a foreign port first. Thus, a ship embarking in Florida for a Caribbean cruise has to visit, say, the Bahamas, before entering another US port. There are exceptions, for example a British ship operating a fly-cruise for British passengers out of New York can visit Boston before crossing the Atlantic. Cruises to Hawaii out of Los Angeles have long visited Ensenada in Mexico.

A new Jones Act, ratified in 2006 by the Bush administration, has resulted in some lightening of the restrictions. Cabotage has limited the availability of US–US cruises that do not have to enter a foreign port. Given the huge amount of continental United States coast line, this does limit choice for the passenger. Norwegian Cruise Line (NCL) founded a subsidiary, NCL (America) in 2004 to offer Hawaiian cruises that did not need to put into foreign ports, as the vessels deployed, *Pride of America* and *Pride of Aloha* (ex-*Norwegian Sky*), were US-flagged. However, in 2008 *Pride of Hawaii* became *Norwegian Jade* and *Pride of Aloha* reverted to *Norwegian Sky* when NCL withdrew from the operation, citing profitability problems.

As shown below, very few ships are registered in the US and carry the Jones Act proportion of US crews: out of a sample of 123 North American market ships over 30,000 GRT, only three were registered in the USA.

Bahamas	47
Italy *	12
Malta**	11
Marshall islands	3
Netherlands ***	12
Panama	20
UK/Bermuda/Gibraltar ****	17
USA	3

Figure 4: Flag Registration of Vessels in the US Cruise Market

*   all Costa Ships (Carnival Group) are registered in Italy.

**   all Celebrity and Azamara vessels are registered in Malta.

***   all Holland America ships (Carnival Group) are registered in the Netherlands.

**** all Princess & Cunard ships (Carnival Group) have traditionally been registered in the UK or the Crown Colonies of Bermuda and Gibraltar.

Whilst many of the major cruise companies that operate in the US market have offices in the US, it is often the case that the companies themselves are incorporated outside the US, thus limiting their US tax liabilities.

There is a paradox in that a cruise of, say, 90+ per cent US passengers, providing North American entertainment and food, will often be on a ship registered outside the US, operated by a company incorporated outside the US and with a crew that may contain only a handful of US members. To all intents and purposes it is an American cruise, but one has to wonder how the US economy benefits?

Registering a ship under a particular flag puts the ship under the legal jurisdiction of that country, although it in no way removes the need for the ship to comply with the safety regulations of the country whose port it is visiting. In July 2001, for example, a ship arrived at Dover, UK, on part of a world cruise, but was prevented from sailing for breaching safety and hygiene inspections. Following further inspection by a team of official surveyors, she was eventually released from detention and allowed to sail, without passengers, on a single voyage to Piraeus, from where she eventually sailed for scrapping.

The US Coastguard and hygiene authorities are very strict about ensuring that vessels leaving US ports comply with US regulations. In 2006, Coastguard officers removed the captain from a large US market ship after he failed a breath-alcohol test during a routine safety inspection. The ship delayed its departure from Seattle until a new captain was located. The captain pleaded guilty to operating a ship while under the influence of alcohol, paid a fine of $15,000, was placed on probation for one year and was banned from entering US waters as an employee of any commercial vessel for the same period.

It is not only the ships that are flagged abroad. Many of the major North American cruise market operators are also registered abroad for tax reasons. As an interesting sideline, many of the P&O/Princess ships that were previously registered in the UK have had their registrations switched to the British Crown Colony of Bermuda, for the regulations of that country allow the captain to conduct on-board weddings whilst UK regulations do not, and on-board weddings are a source of revenue for the cruise companies.

OPENING UP THE NORTH AMERICAN MARKET

Whilst not initially promoted as the type of cruise vacation we know today, the US shipping industry provided a number of 'cruise' opportunities from the 1920s onwards. There were, for example, regular Matson Line sailings to Hawaii and back. The founder, Captain William Matson, had begun a shipping service between California and Hawaii in 1882 with the schooner *Emma Claudina*. The Matson Navigation Company was incorporated in 1901, and the first passenger-ship sailing was made by the steamer *Lurline* in 1908.

The fleet grew, and in 1927 a new liner, *Malolo*, the most lavish yet seen on the west coast of the US, joined the fleet. Matson took over his rival, Los Angeles

The Church of Scientology's *Freewinds* at Barbados.

Steamship Company, which had carried more passengers to Hawaii in 1927 than he had, and expanded operation with three larger, faster, more luxurious ships, *Mariposa*, *Monterey* and *Lurline*, which were all delivered in the early 1930s. They were long-lived ships, which offered both line voyages and cruises to and from the islands to a growing North American cruise market.

In addition to longer voyages to the Hawaiian Islands, other companies had regular services from the eastern seaboard and Gulf ports up and down the coast and into the Caribbean. Regular services also ran from the east through the Panama Canal. The Panama Line offered cruise-type round-trip voyages on the *Panama*, the *Ancon* and the *Christobal* well into the 1960s. Naturally it took far longer than by air, but the 14-night voyage was a relaxing way to travel from New York to the Canal Zone. Before regular air services developed after the Second World War, there were thriving west and east coast inter-costal services. A similar situation was found in the UK, where coastal passenger services lasted into the 1950s. Today, the Norwegian Coastal Voyage is a reminder of the days when coastal steamers provided an important transportation link.

In the 1930s, a typical example of the coastal voyage was the Clyde Mallory service from Jacksonville, Florida, to New York via Charleston, South Carolina. The ship left Jacksonville on a Friday and arrived in New York on a Monday, with the 600 passengers paying as little as $37.50 each way. Whilst these were primarily line voyages, they became increasing regarded as cruises by those who wanted a sea-going vacation. The company also offered voyages to Cuba and up the St Lawrence. Initially intended for those who were seeking an alternative to railroad or bus travel, the voyages made for an ideal short cruise and soon began to be marketed as such.

A little-known cruise opportunity was provided by the Alaska Steamship Company (the Alaska Line). Like its famous European – and still functioning counterpart (Norwegian Coastal Voyage) – the line linked the various Alaskan settlements with Seattle. By 1928, a number of vessels, including *Alaska*, *Aleutian*,

Yukon, *Alameda*, *Northwestern* and *Victoria*, were operating. In 1936, the *Baranof*, the ex-Grace Lines liner, *Santa Elis*, joined the fleet. By the 1950s, only the *Alaska*, *Aleutian* and *Baranof* were still operating, and a ship named *Denali* made the last passenger run for the company in late September 1954. After that, the company survived as a freighter firm until 1971.

The Bergen Line employed their small steamer, *Meteor*, in Alaska during 1970 and 1971. On 22 May 1971, she caught fire off Vancouver. All the passengers were rescued, but thirty-two of the crew perished. *Meteor* did not sink, was subsequently sold and had a further long career in the Mediterranean. The growth in Alaskan cruising in the later years of the twentieth century and into the twenty-first is covered later.

THE BERMUDA RUN AND THE HONEYMOON SHIPS

For those who lived in the vicinity of New York, the service provided by the British Furness Bermuda Line offered an excellent opportunity for a short cruise. Just as Norway was a popular cruising destination for early UK cruises due to its proximity to the British Isles, so Bermuda was attractive to those on the eastern seaboard of the US. Christopher Furness, a renowned UK shipowner, had bought a British and a Canadian company in the New York–West Indies trade in 1919 and 1920 respectively. Amalgamating the companies as the Bermuda and West Indies Steamship Company (known as Furness Bermuda Line) as part of the Furness Withy Company of London, he exploited prohibition with services on the lucrative New York–Bermuda run.

Initially the *Fort Victoria* (ex-*Willochra*) was acquired in 1919, and operated on the service until 1929. On 18 December of that year, as she was leaving New York in fog, she was rammed by the inbound *Alonquin*. No lives were lost, but the ship sank. The introduction of the *Bermuda* in the late 1920s brought new standards of luxury to the route, with 616 of the 619 passengers travelling first class. The *Bermuda* caught fire and was destroyed in 1931, just after the introduction of a

A builder's model of Furness Bemuda's *Queen of Bermuda* on board Fred Olsen Cruise Line's *Braemar*.

larger vessel, the *Monarch of Bermuda*. This 1931-built ship, which replaced the ill-fated *Bermuda* of 1927, and her younger sister, the 1933 *Queen of Bermuda*, became known as the 'honeymoon ships'.

Taking 42 hours for the twice-weekly New York–Hamilton run, they were very popular with the newly married, who could enjoy both a cruise and a stay on Bermuda as their honeymoon. The service lasted until 1966, although short cruises to Bermuda have remained popular. Indeed, in the 1960s there were a number of smaller companies solely engaged in the US–Bermuda cruise market. Bermuda has continued to be a popular destination for short cruises out of US ports, especially New York, and nearly all of the major companies have a vessel in this market. From the 1960s onward, Hamilton, Bermuda, became a very busy cruise port.

Down to the Caribbean

The Caribbean trade and the US administered islands in the region, plus the US influence in Cuba, generated a great deal of business for both US and foreign shipping firms. The Royal Mail Line service has already been mentioned, but there were many opportunities to use the services to Puerto Rico, the Virgin Islands and Cuba as a cruise vacation.

Ward Line operated a New York–Havana service with its 1930-built *Morro Castle* and her sister, *Oriente*. As the *Morro Castle* was returning to New York on 8 September 1934, tragedy struck. Off the New Jersey coast that night, the captain suffered a fatal heart attack, and then fire broke out. With the command structure disrupted the fire took hold, and 137 lives were lost. An inquiry found that the ship was badly equipped and manned by a poorly trained crew. The disaster led to lawsuits totalling $13.5 million – a staggering amount for those days.

The New York & Porto Rico Steamship Company linked continental US with its important and strategic Caribbean possession. In 1907, together with Clyde, Mallory and Ward Lines, it became part of the Atlantic, Gulf & West Indies Steamship Company, later known as Agwilines. The Porto Rico operation began to offer cruises in the 1930s using the *Coamo* and the *Borinquen*. The former was torpedoed and sunk in 1942, but the latter went on to have a long life, firstly as Bull Line's *Puerto Rico*, on her original route, and then as the *Arosa Star* for the Swiss-owned Arosa Lines. In this role she operated in the Mediterranean, across the Atlantic and even continued cruising to the Caribbean out of the US. In 1960, with the demise of Arosa Line, she returned to the US and cruised out of Miami until 1968 as the *Bahama Star* for Eastern Steamship Lines. *Bahama Star* was one of the ships that, in the early days, contributed to the growth of Miami as a major cruise base port.

Enter the Germans

The 1930s were the heyday of the Atlantic liner trade, with ships such as the *Normandie*, *Queen Mary*, *Bremen* and *Rex* becoming household names on both sides of the Atlantic, bringing to sea travel a degree of luxury hitherto unknown.

Brilliance of the Seas in Caribbean surroundings.

Royal Princess in the Panama
Canal in the early 1990s.
(Courtesy Princess Cruises)

For the first time, ships were airy and light with huge public rooms for all classes, and, consequently, were well-equipped to undertake periodic pleasure cruises in addition to their liner trade duties. In 1938, the French Line's *Normandie*, 83 000 GRT and considered by many to be the most beautiful ship ever built, undertook a 22-day New York–Rio de Janeiro–New York cruise, with ticket prices ranging from $395 to $8,600.

The German government under Adolf Hitler used cruising as a means of rewarding loyal workers. The KdF (Kraft durch Freude/Strength through Joy) cruise operation was directly controlled by the propaganda ministry of the Third Reich. The organisation ran an all-German cruise operation that offered inexpensive vacations for workers and, especially, Nazi Party members. Whilst the organisation commenced using recently constructed German tonnage from the recognised German shipping companies, by 1938/39 they had also placed in service the 25,000-GRT ships *Wilhelm Gustloff* and *Robert Ley*, these ships becoming the first specially commissioned cruise vessels to enter service for any nationality. Both were sunk with great loss of life towards the end of the Second World War, but they became the prototype for the purpose-built cruise ships of

today. All 1,465 passengers had outside cabins – a provision not repeated until the *Royal Princess* of 1984.

These ships are also important in to the history of the industry in that they offered, for the first time, cruise vacations to the middle and working classes. Hitherto, cruising was the preserve of the wealthy.

Paradoxically, the outbreak of war in Europe in 1939 provided the domestic US cruise market with a boost, as British and German passenger ships disappeared from the market into war work, leaving the Caribbean market particularly free for US-flagged vessels. Foremost amongst these was the new flagship of United States Lines, *America*, which entered service in 1940. Intended as a trans-Atlantic liner, she was delivered on 2 June 1940 and made her first New York–West Indies cruise on 10 August. Her older consorts, *Washington* and *Manhattan*, were also employed in cruising, until the attack on Pearl Harbour when all three ships became troop transports.

Once the US was in the war, all thoughts of cruising vanished, and the one-time pleasure ships were converted to the more serious business of transporting millions of US and Allied troops across the Atlantic and the Pacific.

CHAPTER TWO

Post-War US Cruising

NEW SHIPS FOR NEW TIMES

As the liner trade declined as a result of encroaching air travel for the masses, a new generation of ships were purpose-built for cruising. With Europe and Asia ravaged by war, it was only within the US that a mass market for cruising remained feasible. In January 1947, the first US-registered ship to commence post-Second World War cruising out of New York was the 9,100-GRT *Santa Rosa*, but perhaps the benchmark for this new type of ship was set by Cunard's *Caronia* of 1948. Although she carried two classes, she was intended for a joint cruising and liner service career, and was designed to appeal especially to US cruise passengers.

Caronia, 34,183 GRT, was launched in 1948, and was a beacon of luxury in an austere post-war Britain. Known as the Green Goddess, because of the seven shades of green paint on her hull (designed to reflect the heat of the sun in the days before air conditioning), she was aimed primarily at the wealthier end of the North American cruise market and was a supreme example of the shipbuilder's art, her superb interiors contributing to her enormous popularity for many years. She developed an extremely loyal following, and one of her lady guests lived aboard almost continuously for fourteen years: it is said that *Caronia*'s captain used to wait, with bated breath, for an invitation to dine at her table!

She was deployed on longer cruises, and her Cunard career lasted until 1968, by which time she had been out-classed by newer vessels. She was fated to become the down-market *Caribia*. Beset by fire and maintenance problems, she was virtually abandoned at a berth in New York (Bill Miller reports that she was given a parking ticket by the NYPD), then on her way to Taiwan for scrapping in 1974 she broke her tow and was wrecked off Guam. She broke into three and was cut up where she lay; a sad end to a beautiful ship.

On her maiden entry to New York in 1965, the 39,000-GRT *Oceanic* of Home Lines was referred to as 'the ship of tomorrow'. Although she had been designed originally as a two-class trans-Atlantic liner for the Northern Europe–North America (St Lawrence) service, she was eventually completed as a cruise ship for the US

market and carried 1,601 cruise guests. Every cabin on the ship was equipped with en-suite facilities and her two swimming pools could be covered by a magrodome. North Americans clambered for cruises on her and she was fully booked years ahead for her weekly New York–Nassau cruises. So successful was her design that, after a number of name changes, she traded until recently under her original name in the Spanish market for Pullmantur Cruises, a company acquired by Royal Caribbean in 2007. Today, she is named *Peaceboat*.

Home Lines, later acquired by Holland America, also operated the 42,000-GRT *Homeric*, which later became *Westerdam* and *Atlantic* before being passed on, in 1988, to Premier Cruises as the *Starship Atlantic*. Premier Cruises had acquired *Oceanic*, as *Starship Oceanic* in 1985. *Homeric*, ex-*Westerdam*, eventually became *Costa Europa* before being transferred, in 2009, to Thomson Cruises for a ten-year charter.

By the 1960s, many of the liner companies were operating cruises for the North American market. Swedish America, Cunard, Costa, Home Lines and a host of others offered week-long cruises out of New York to Bermuda and other nearby destinations using their Atlantic liners. Bermuda was a popular destination. Many of these cruises were described in a series of letters sent by a veteran guest to his travel agent and published by the Ocean Liner Society as the Dear Denny letters in the publication *Sealines*.

The Alcoa Steamship Company (Alcoa being the Aluminium Company of America), had begun a cruise operation using the chartered *Acadia*, *St John* and *Evangeline* at a less than auspicious time – early 1941. Once the US entered the war in December of that year, this US–Bermuda and Caribbean cruise operation was suspended. After the war, the company chartered the 5,100-GRT *George Washington* for use on the Bermuda run, and this ship was able to enter service before the Furness Bermuda operation could restart. Sadly for the company, the ship was old, having been built in 1924, and in 1948 the service was withdrawn as newer vessels arrived to compete.

Delta Line's classic *Del Mar*, *Del Norte* and *Del Sud* were introduced in 1946 as guest/cargo liners on the New Orleans, St Thomas, Rio and Buenos Aires run.

The 'Ship of Tomorrow', *Oceanic* in Pullmantur service at Livorno.

One of the earlier NCL ships, *Starward* became the *Bolero* in the European market.

Westerdam showing her length.

Striking ships they were, and in the early 1960s were still being advertised as cruise ships, offering extended South American vacations. Unfortunately, there were too few who could afford the time, even though the trip cost only $9 per day, and the ships ceased to carry passengers in 1967.

The Hawaiian–Textron Lines chartered the converted ex-troopship, *La Guardia*, from the parent Textron Company in order to operate an Hawaiian cruise service to undercut Matson Lines. Renamed *Leilani* (Hawaiian for lovely flower), she entered service in January 1957 but was beset with problems, including an outbreak of food poisoning. Eventually the ship was laid up in 1958, before being sold as *President Roosevelt* to American President Lines, a company which operated the ship on Pacific services with fleet-sisters *President Cleveland* and *President Wilson*

President Roosevelt was rebuilt as a luxury 456-berth vessel for far eastern and world cruising and was re-named *Atlantis*. In 1972, she was sold to Eastern Steamship Lines as *Emerald Seas*. This company was taken over by Admiral Cruises and finally by Royal Caribbean. The ship was laid up, and although many plans were made for her, she went through a series of name changes and was eventually sold to Greek interests as *Emerald Seas*. *President Cleveland* and *President Wilson* ended their active careers as full-time cruise ships and were laid up in 1973.

The Growth Continues

Traditional liner companies, such as Matson Lines, Grace Lines and American President Lines, all started to focus on cruising. Whilst the advent of jet travel sounded the death knell for the liner, paradoxically it helped to open up cruising. In

The *Emerald* sailed as the *Regent Rainbow*, but before rebuilding was the elegant Grace Line's *Santa Rosa*.

the 1960s New York was a major cruise port, with the Atlantic liner trade declining but the cruise market expanding. There were not enough suitable vessels available, and more and more older ships were being rebuilt to suit the cruise trade. The beautiful *Victoria*, introduced by Icres Lines in 1959 for Caribbean cruising, was a rebuild of the *Dunnottar Castle* of 1936. She was originally an intermediate mail ship of the Union-Castle Line, engaged in the mail and liner service from the UK to southern Africa. After the conversion, it was difficult to see anything of the original ship. As *Princess Victoria*, she was still cruising in the Mediterranean until well into the first decade of the twenty-first century.

Grace Line's *Santa Rosa* and *Santa Paula* of 1932 were operated on the New York–Caribbean service of the company. They were well suited to cruising, and it was *Santa Rosa* that operated the first post-war cruise out of New York on 8 February 1947. After she was sold to Greek owners in 1960, she ended her life playing the salvaged *Titanic* in the film *Raise the Titanic*, based on the Clive Cussler novel of the same title. Apparently the movie cost so much that it was said at the time that, rather than raising the *Titanic*, it might have been cheaper to lower the Atlantic!

The new *Santa Rosa* and *Santa Paula* of 1957 and 1958 operated on the same route, but were laid up in 1971 after Grace Line became Presidential-Grace Lines. *Santa Paula* became a floating hotel in Kuwait, whilst *Santa Rosa* was rebuilt after a twenty-year lay up. She became the rather awkward looking *Regent Rainbow* for Regency Cruises, and operated in this role within the US market until Regency Cruises failed in 1995. She was sold to Louis Cruise Lines of Cyprus in 1997, renamed *Emerald*, and was then leased to Thomson Cruises for UK market operations. At the time of writing, her scrapping was imminent. There were plans in the 1980s to convert the four cargo/guest liners of the *Santa Magdalena* class into South Pacific cruise ships, but this never came to fruition.

Moore–McCormack was another US shipping company that used cruising to reinvigorate its operations. In the late 1920s the company had introduced the largest passenger liners yet built in the USA, the 20,000+ GRT *Argentina*, *Brazil* and *Uruguay*. With twin funnels (smokestacks) – one of which was a dummy – they plied their trade from New York to San Francisco, via Cuba, the Panama Canal and Mexico, or down to South America. All three survived the war, and by 1952 the company was advertising the service as '38-day cruises to South America – the vacation you had always promised yourself'. But the three ships were too old and were laid up in the mid-1950s.

The company went on to introduce two new long-lived vessels in 1958. They were the new *Brasil* and *Argentina*: a little smaller at 15,200 GRT, they were designed as line/cruise ships for the New York–Buenos Aires route and were very modern in appearance. After refits in 1963, the ships began to sail in earnest, offering cruises to Scandinavia, Southern Europe and Africa. In the face of increasing airline competition, however, the ships were sold in 1969 to Holland America as the *Volendam* and the *Veendam*. Since then they have had a number of name changes.

Volendam on a rainy day in Alaska.

Far from the Caribbean, *Jewel of the Seas* leaves Bergen.

Volendam became the *Monarch Sun* for a time, and then *Volendam* again. She then spent time as the *Island Sun, Liberte, Canada Star* then *Queen of Bermuda*, before becoming the *Enchanted Seas* for Commodore Cruise Line. *Veendam* had a similar career becoming the *Brasil* (the original name of her sister) for a time in 1974, then *Veendam* again followed by *Monarch Star, Veendam* (again) then *Bermuda Star* and finally, in 1990, when the Bermuda Star Line was acquired by Commodore Cruise Line, she became the *Enchanted Isle*.

Commodore Cruise Line was founded in 1968 by Florida hotelier, Sandy Chobol, and Edwin Stephan (later of Royal Caribbean). Chobol had earlier operated the *Princess Leopoldina* for a season out of Florida. In 1968, the first vessel chartered by the fledgling company was the new *Bohème*, one of a series of four car ferries then under construction in Finland. She was redesigned as a cruise ship, and for some three years she operated 7-night trips out of Miami. From 1973–1976, *Bohème* was joined by the Fred Olsen car ferry *Bolero*, which also ran a service from Portland, Maine, USA and Yarmouth, Nova Scotia during the summer. *Bolero* was replaced by *Caribe 1* (not to be confused with the ex-*Caronia*), which had been the Greek Line's *Olympia* and which was also operated as a ferry between the US and Canada in the peak summer months. She was used on 7-night, 4-island trips to Montego Bay, Port Antonio, Puerto Plata and Port-au-Prince.

One survivor from the liner trade that could be seen in Aruba well into 2003 was *Southern Cross* of the British Shaw Savill Line. Built by Harland & Wolff, Belfast, in 1955 for a new round-the-world passenger service, she carried 1,100 passengers in one class and was one of the pioneers of the engines-aft layout. Her continuous circuits from Southampton took 76 days to complete and called at Trinidad, Curacao, the Panama Canal, Tahiti, Fiji, Wellington, Auckland, Sydney, Melbourne, Fremantle, Durban, Capetown, Las Palmas and back to Southampton. From 1968, she ran cruises between her regular circumnavigations. Escalating costs and competition from air travel caused her withdrawal in 1971, and she was laid up in the River Fal for two years before being sold to Greek interests in 1973.

She then reappeared in service for Ulysses Line in 1975 as *Calypso*, and in 1980 was sold to Western Cruise Lines and renamed *Azure Seas*. The company later became Admiral Cruise Line, eventually being taken over by Royal Caribbean. However, *Azure Seas* was sold to Dolphin Cruise Line in 1991, and renamed *Ocean Breeze*. Dolphin later became part of Premier Cruises, and the dark blue Premier colours were applied, although in 1999 *Ocean Breeze* carried the dual identity of *Imperial Majesty* on her stern whilst under charter to Majesty Cruise Line for short trips out of Fort Lauderdale. Finally, this great old lady succumbed to the breakers in 2003.

THE SCANDINAVIAN INFLUENCE

Efjohn, Royal Caribbean, Royal Viking, Norwegian Cruise Line and Flagship Lines all had their roots in Scandinavia, in particular Norway. Given the Scandinavian tradition of seafaring, as exemplified by the Vikings, this should be no surprise. The companies have been very successful in the North American market, with the exception of Flagship Lines. Their *Viking Princess* cruised in the Caribbean area from 1964 until 8 April 1966, when she caught fire off Cuba. Two passengers were lost in the blaze, and the ship was scrapped in Spain.

Immigration to the US from the Scandinavian countries of Sweden, Norway, Denmark, and Finland increased dramatically in the late nineteenth century, due to mounting economic pressures and overpopulation. The Homestead Act of 1862, which gave free land to settlers who developed it for at least five years, was a particular magnet for Norwegians, Danes, and Swedes and Finns. Though not as numerous as German or Irish immigrants, Scandinavians still arrived in massive numbers. 1,000,000 Swedes (1868–1914); 800,000 Norwegians (1825–1925); 300,000 Danes (1820–1920), and 230,000 Finns (1890–1924) entered the USA and provided strong links to their homelands, which may account for the preponderance of Scandinavian influence in the current North American cruise market.

In the 1990s, Commodore Cruise Line was bought by the Scandinavian company Effjohn International: Effjohn were the owners of Silja Line and Sally Line, amongst others, and had bought the Bermuda Star Line the year before, merging its two ships into Commodore under the names *Enchanted Isle* and *Enchanted Seas*. These had originally been built in 1958 as the *Argentina* and *Brasil* of Moore–McCormack (see earlier). *Caribe I* was sold to Regal Cruise Line as *Regal Empress*. In 1995, Effjohn sold Commodore to New York-based JeMJ Financial Services, and they added the ex-Soviet vessel *Enchanted Capri* to the fleet, sailing out of New Orleans to join the *Enchanted Isle*. *Enchanted Sun,* built as *Castalia*, also joined the fleet.

In 1999, Commodore resurrected an earlier brand, Crown Cruise Line, which had previously been owned and operated by Effjohn from 1987–1997. The intention was to equip the new company with the modern ships that the cruising public were demanding. The *Crown Dynasty* was re-acquired for cruises to Bermuda, but was sold to Fred Olsen Cruises in 2001 and now operates as *Braemar* in the UK market. Commodore ceased operations in 2000, as did Premier Cruises and Canaveral Cruise Lines.

CHAPTER THREE

In US Waters – Cruising to Hawaii and Alaska

Whilst the Caribbean often springs to mind when thinking about the North American cruise market, there are two other areas near to North America that have also played a major role in the development of the industry: Hawaii and Alaska.

One of the earliest entrants to Pacific cruising was a company that was synonymous with the US–Hawaii liner trade: Matson Line.

HAWAIIAN CRUISING

The roots of Matson Line went back to the late nineteenth century. The company was responsible for introducing mass tourism to Hawaii, with the opening of the Moana Hotel and the famous Royal Hawaiian Hotel in Waikiki. These hotels supplemented the guest shipping operations of the company, especially after the 1926 take over of the Oceanic Steamship Company with three trans-Pacific liners. From the early twentieth century through the 1970s, Matson liners sailed from the west coast ports of San Francisco and Los Angeles to Honolulu and points beyond, including Australia and New Zealand. From the late 1920s onwards, the company's white ships provided not only a regular service to Hawaii but a superb cruising opportunity. The *Malolo* (re-christened *Matsonia*), *Lurline*, *Mariposa* and *Monterey* were elegant classic ocean liners that provided an excellent cruise experience. Even when the company was forced out of cruising in the 1970s, the ships themselves found new owners.

Matsonia ended her commercial service in 1973, although she was not sent for scrap until 1977 and, as Chandris's *Queen Frederica*, was one of the vessels that began the growth in British fly cruising, operating short Mediterranean cruises linked to charter flights from what was then the little-known airport of London Gatwick. *Lurline* became the *Ellenis* (also Chandris), *Mariposa* went to Home Lines as the cruise ship *Homeric* in 1953 and lasted until 1974. The *Monterey* of 1932 was renamed *Matsonia* and then *Lurline*, before becoming the *Britanis* of Chandris in 1970.

In 1987 and 1988, Aloha Pacific Cruises operated the ex-Matson Liner *Monterey*. The company collapsed after a major food poisoning incident. Despite a $40 million refurbishment, the Federal Drug Administration (FDA) warned that the vessel was not fit to sail in September 1988, but sail she did. Following the incident she was laid up and eventually purchased by the Mediterranean Shipping Company.

After the Second World War, American Export Lines had introduced two beautiful ships for the Mediterranean–US liner route. *Independence* and *Constitution*, at just over 30,000 GRT apiece, were displaced from the regular liner trade by aircraft, but found a new role cruising. Initially they operated three-week-long cruises from New York to the Mediterranean, and back. In 1968, *Independence* was reconfigured for one-class cruising. Marketed as 'Go–Go Cruises' and with a huge face of Jean Harlow on her hull, she looked surreal. Prices were low, just $98 for a 7-day cruise, but food was extra. The venture failed, and by 1970 both ships were laid up. However, both were to have a new lease of life in the Pacific.

Constitution was laid up until 1974, when she was sold to the C.Y. Tung group and renamed *Oceanic Constitution*. She remained laid up in Hong Kong until Tung started American Hawaii Cruises in 1980, operating a 7-day cruise out of Honolulu. The operation was successful, and *Constitution* regained her original name and entered service in 1982 following a substantial refurbishment. When it became too expensive to bring her up to the mandatory SOLAS (Safety of Life At Sea) standards, she was sold for scrap in 1997, but sank in the Pacific whilst under tow to the Far East.

Independence was laid up until 1974, when she too was sold to the C.Y. Tung group and renamed *Oceanic Independence*. She was briefly used for cruising, but then laid up in Hong Kong in 1976 as *Sea Luck I*. When Tung started American Hawaii Cruises in 1980, *Sea Luck I*, again renamed *Oceanic Independence*, operated 7-day cruises out of Honolulu. An American subsidiary had been created, allowing the ship to be US-flagged. The service was a success. In 1987, the cruise line was sold by Tung group for $20 million. American Hawaii Cruises filed for bankruptcy in 2001, following poor trading in the wake of the September 11th terrorist attacks.

In February 2003, *Independence* was sold at auction for $4 million to Norwegian Cruise Line (NCL), which also acquired *United States*. At this time, NCL received permission to create US-flagged cruise operation, to be named NCL America. (As has been said, US flagging is a valuable competitive advantage, as cabotage prohibits non-US lines from transporting passengers from one US port to another without stopping at a foreign port, and in particular it permits 7-day Hawaiian cruises. As US flagging requires US-built ships, no other major cruise operation is US-flagged.) In fact, cabotage was one of the issues that bedevilled the expansion of the US market as very few of the vessels were US flagged.

In mid-2006, *Independence* was renamed *Oceanic*, despite the fact that there was already a ship of that name operating for Pullmantur Cruises. Scrapping was rumoured. In July 2007, Norwegian Cruise Line announced that *Oceanic* had been sold, with later reports claiming the ship had been purchased by an American company. She was towed out of San Francisco Bay on 8 February 2008, with her final destination revealed to be Singapore, but this was then changed to Dubai and then perhaps a scrapyard in India or Bangladesh. Due to a complaint filed by the US Environmental Protection Agency, her removal had been stopped, but she was towed away nonetheless and Global Marketing Systems, the final owners of the ship, were fined $518,500 for exporting the ship for scrap without prior removal of asbestos and polychlorinated biphenyls.

Whilst much of the US market growth had been in the Caribbean, the Pacific seaboard had also seen growth.

ALASKAN CRUISING

One home-grown area of US cruising that has seen massive growth has been Alaska. Alaskan cruising had been mainly in the hands of the regular steamships of the Alaska Steamship Company up to 1954 (see earlier). The Canadian National Railway (CN) also operated between Vancouver and Alaska and introduced a cruise ferry, *Prince George*, in 1946. Laid up in the 1980s, she lingered on as either an accommodation ship or in lay up until she caught fire in 1995 and sank on her way to the breakers.

However, in 1971 Holland America Line purchased controlling interest in the Alaska-based Westours and began the company's move into the Alaskan market, which was just then transforming from the era of the smaller, coastal, Canadian-owned ships to the larger multinational lines such as the British P&O company that were also developing the area.

In 1975, the *Prinsendam* became the first Holland America Line ship to sail the Inside Passage, and in 1976 she was joined on the Alaskan run by *Veendam*. In October of 1980, a fire broke out on the *Prinsendam* while she was sailing south of Yakutat. All 520 passengers and crew were safely evacuated by the Coastguard and the ship placed under tow, but she capsized and sank west of Sitka. Her sinking in the Gulf of Alaska is dealt with in greater detail in the section on Holland America Line, which follows a little later.

One of the ships chosen to replace the *Prinsendam* on the rapidly expanding Alaska summer run was the Holland America flagship *Rotterdam*. After 1983, she sailed regularly in the Inside Passage.

One of the serious issues relating to cruising, especially in environmentally sensitive areas such as Alaska, is that of pollution – in particular, the discharge of oil products. In 2008, the Alaskan Press reported at least twenty-two cases of oil and wastewater discharges that broke state laws. The Alaskan authorities impose strict regulations and harsh penalties on these issues. To be fair to the cruise operators, pollution control on board cruise vessels is much improved, and the major companies appear to take their responsibilities very seriously.

It was in Alaskan waters that one of the most damaging oil spillage incidents occurred, when the oil spillage of the tanker *Exxon Valdez* occurred in Prince William Sound on 24 March 1989. Although the spillage was far down on the list of the world's largest oil spills in terms of volume released, the Sound's remote location, accessible only by helicopter and boat, made both the response of the government and industry difficult, and severely taxed the pre-existing plans for response. The vessel spilled 10.8 million US gallons (about 40 million litres) of crude oil from Prudoe Bay into the sea, and the oil eventually covered 11,000 square miles (28,000 square km) of ocean in a region that was a habitat for a large variety of wildlife.

Princess Cruises also expanded into Alaska, and both Princess and Holland America (now both Carnival Companies) operated not only ships, but hotels and even rail tours in the state. To illustrate the integrated nature of Alaskan cruising, a case study was prepared by Roger Cartwright for a book detailing the cruise operations of P&O, relating to the Princess operation in Alaska. The study is reproduced below:

PRINCESS IN ALASKA

Princess had been one of the first companies to expand into Alaska, and P&O had used the *Arcadia* of 1954 in the area. Both Princess and Holland America expanded Alaskan operations to include not only cruises, but stays in their own lodges and even acquired their own sightseeing vehicles and trains. For the cruise guest this meant a seamless means of seeing one of the last accessible wildernesses. Air flights from within North America or further afield are arranged at the same time as the cruise is booked. Hotel stays where necessary, in cities such as Seattle or Vancouver, are part of the package for those travelling long distances.

The Princess Alaskan operation is exceptionally well organised (as is that offered by Holland America). Passengers have the options of taking just a cruise, or adding on a Rocky Mountains or Alaskan land tour, or indeed taking both tours. The Rocky Mountain land tours utilise the Rocky Mountaineer train between Jasper and Vancouver, with a pre-train coach travel and an overnight stop in Kamloops between Jasper and Vancouver. The train enables passengers to experience the full grandeur of the Rocky Mountains.

Alaska Rail hauling Princess dome cars en route to joining a Princess cruise ship in Wittier.

In Alaska, Princess offers a variety of land tours based on the five lodges that the company operates: Fairbanks; Denali; Mount McKinley; Copper River and Kenai Wilderness lodges. Each lodge comprises comfortable rooms, shops and a variety of diners and restaurants. Those feeling energetic can walk the trails surrounding the lodges and look out for bears, moose, bald eagles etc. The tours use buses and trains to transport passengers between the lodges. The whole exercise is an exemplar in logistics.

Whether on a bus or a train before arriving at the next lodge, the guest receives an envelope containing details of the lodge they are travelling to, room keys and details of the next day's activities or journey. Upon arriving in Alaska the guest leaves a suitcase with Princess for the company to transfer to the ship, and keeps another case for the land tour. This case is collected and delivered to and from the room in the lodge. Thus, all the guest needs to travel with is a hand tote and a camera.

The staff at the lodges is split between hotel staff and 'Princess Outfitters', the latter looking after transfers and excursions from the lodge etc. The land tour case is delivered directly to the ship, and on arrival in a stateroom the guest finds their entire luggage waiting for them. Check in for the cruise is undertaken on the final bus or train leg, so that it is literally straight off the bus or train, through security, and onto the ship.

Princess, Holland America, Celebrity and Royal Caribbean all operate their own train carriages. For the Fairbanks–Denali journey, on the Denali Express all the companies' carriages operate in the same train pulled by Alaska Rail locomotives. The double-deck dome cars operated by Princess provide an upstairs seat for each guest, with a dining section in the lower portion of the carriage. On some journeys between Mount McKinley and the berth at Whittier, single-deck panoramic cars converted by Alaska Rail from the stock of the Florida Fun Train are used. Due to the large loading gauge of US railroads, the view from these dome cars is superb. Each car has its own guide and bartender. It is difficult to imagine a more relaxing method of seeing Alaska. With control of the lodges and the transportation, Princess is able to provide a seamless experience of guaranteed quality.

CHAPTER FOUR

From Liners to Cruise Ships

The *France* and *Empress of Canada* of 1960, together with the *Galileo Galilei* and *Gugliemo Marcon* of 1961, were perhaps the last vessels to be designed as true trans-Atlantic liners, and even then *France* began cruising early on in her career. The *QE2* of 1967, the 1965 Swedish America vessel, *Kungsholm*, and the 1964 and 1972 semi-sisters *Sagafjord* and *Vistafjord* of Norwegian America, were designed with cruising in mind from the outset.

In the penultimate week of Christmas 1968, the berths in New York's Luxury Liner's Row that in a previous decade would have been packed with the great trans-Atlantic liners on their US–Europe services, were now filled up with nine cruise ships preparing for Christmas and New Year cruises; *Gripsholm* of Swedish America, Canadian Pacific's *Empress of Canada*, *Queen Anna Maria* (Greek Line), *Leonardo da Vinci*, *Victoria*, *Oceanic* and *Homeric*. Even the mighty *United States* and *France* were going cruising over the holiday period. The days of the liner voyage were really almost over, and a new era was beginning.

One of those who saw the opportunities at this time was John Chandris from Greece, and his company was to acquire many ex-liners for operations in both the American and European markets. His insignia lives on today in the white X funnel decoration of the ships operated by Celebrity Cruises. Chandris was responsible for the transformation of many old liners into smart new cruise ships.

By 1976, much of the cruise market was being served by specially constructed vessels. In February 1976, the growing port of Miami contained eight cruise ships, most of which were new vessels. Only the *Mardi Gras* of Carnival was previously a liner, and Commodore Cruise Line's *Bolero* (on charter from Fred Olsen) a converted car ferry. The rest – Royal Caribbean's *Song of Norway*, *Nordic Prince*, Norwegian Cruise Line's *Starward*, *Skyward* and *Southward*, and Commodore's *Boheme* – were all designed and built as cruise ships.

CHANDRIS

John D. Chandris pioneered the Greek entry into the US market. He entered guest shipping in the Aegean in 1922 with the steamer *Chimara*. John died at the end of the Second World War but his two sons, Anthony and Dimitri, then living in London, rebuilt the company into the largest of the Greek-owned cruise lines. In 1959, the company bought Union-Castle's *Bloemfontein Castle*, with the intention of inaugurating a service to Australia. Operating under the name of the Greek Australia Line, the company sent the ship to England for refit. She emerged as *Patris*, 18,400 GRT, and made her first voyage from Piraeus, via Suez, to Freemantle, Melbourne and Sydney in November 1959.

The next acquisition was the similarly sized *Brittany*, built in 1952. She was chartered by Chandris in 1960 and began her service from Piraeus, Greece, to Australian ports in 1961. This was the beginning of the company's long association with the Australian migrant and tourist trades. Another purchase was the American *Lurline*, which became the highly popular *Ellinis*. With her, Chandris started their

A reminder of the past – a mural of a Matson Line's vessel docking in Honolulu. The mural adorns the cruise terminal at Honolulu.

Patris, ex-Bloemfontein Castle. (Newall-Dunn Collection)

round-the-world service in 1963. Sailings to Australia went outbound via the Suez (and later South Africa), and then returned via the Panama Canal. In a relatively short time, more and more of the company's business was derived from cruising, and many more ships were converted for Mediterranean cruising, including several ex-UK cross-Channel and Isle of Man ferries.

In 1973, the company began to increase its North American cruise operations. As has been said, Chandris ships were easily identifiable by the large X on their funnels. In Greek, this letter represents the 'chi' sound, a direct link to the name of the owners. Whilst owning many ships, only a few Chandris vessels were dedicated to the North American market, but those that were played an important part in developing the market as we know it today, and are listed below.

Romantica: As the ex-Furness Red Cross liner *Fort Townsend*, she had undertaken some cruising out of New York for the Furness Bermuda operation until her sale to Saudi interests in 1951. She later became the Saudi Royal Yacht. Bought by Chandris in 1960 she was renamed *Romantica*, and whilst the majority of her cruising was in the Mediterranean, she operated short Caribbean cruises out of Aruba in 1968–69.

Brittany: Built in the late 1940s as the *Bretagne* for the French company Transport Maritimes for their Marseilles–South America service, she was acquired by Chandris in 1960 and refitted in early 1961. The French government and unions insisted that her name and many of her French crew be retained, and she was not renamed *Brittany* (the English version of her name) until 1962. Refitted, she began successful cruises to Bermuda and the Bahamas out of New York. Under refit in Greece in April 1963, however, just before her second US season, she caught fire and became a total loss.

Australis/America/Italis: We covered the original career of the United States Lines' *America* earlier in this book. After her sale to Chandris, re-named *Australis*, she did not cruise in the US market. However, she returned to the US in 1978 and was

renamed *America*, having been sold to American (later Venture) Cruise Lines. She was not a success, and there were many complaints about the ship. The service started in May and had failed by August, when Chandris repurchased her. They sold her for $5 million and re-acquired her for $1 million – a tidy profit!

Renamed *Italis* she was sold again in 1980, eventually becoming the *Alferdoss* (Paradise). Laid up, she had major engineering problems and was sold for scrap. However, after an Australian deal to purchase her as a floating hotel fell through in 1992, a Thai company announced their intention to renovate her as a floating hotel in Phuket. Renamed *American Star*, she departed Piraeus on 24 December 1993, but due to extreme weather conditions returned to port the next day. Six days later, on New Year's Eve, she recommenced her journey and passed Gibraltar on 12 January 1994. On 15 January, during a severe storm, she broke loose and remained adrift with four salvage crew still on board.

Several attempts were made to take her under tow again, but they failed. The four crew members were winched off the ship by helicopter and she was left adrift. On 17 January she ran aground off the west coast of Fuerteventura in the Canary Islands, and six months later was declared a total loss. Eventually her stern section collapsed into the sea, and today her bow, part of her forward superstructure and some of her remaining funnel (one was removed much earlier whilst still in service) is still visible but decaying fast. Thus ended a great US liner.

Regina: The former liner, *Panama*, was built by Bethlehem Steel and entered service in 1939, spending the war as the troopship USS *James L. Parker*. Sold to American President Lines, she became their *President Hoover* before her sale to Chandris as the *Regina* in December 1964. Her summers were spent cruising the Mediterranean, whilst in winter she served the American market on 7-day cruises out of Curaçao. Renamed *Regina Prima* in 1972, she was laid up in 1979 and sold for scrap in 1985.

The 1948 *Caronia* – the 'Green Goddess'. (Newall-Dunn Collection)

Zenith at San Juan.

Queen Frederica: The famous Matson liner *Malolo* was acquired by Chandris as the *Queen Frederica* in 1965. Chandris intended that she work in the US market supported by the *Brittany* (see above), before that ship was lost. However, stricter US Coastguard standards introduced in 1968 curtailed her US operations – she had been engaged on short cruises out of New York. She was transferred to Europe and played an important part in the expansion of the UK market before being laid up in 1973 and being destroyed by fire in 1978.

Amerikanis: Built as the Union-Castle intermediate liner *Kenya Castle* for the UK–Africa liner service, she was a classic British liner of the immediate post-war years. Rendered redundant, she was acquired by Chandris in 1967, whose objective was to use her to develop the US market for the company, naming her *Amerikanis*. A highly successful and popular ship, she was chartered to Costa for a time. She cruised out of New York, Port Everglades and San Juan (Puerto Rico). She transferred to Europe in 1993, was laid up in 1996, and was finally broken up in 2001.

Britanis: Another of the Matson Liners that Chandris acquired was *Monterey* of 1932. She was refitted as a cruise ship in 1956–57 and renamed *Matsonia*. After Matson Lines sold the *Lurline*, *Matsonia* became the new (and last *Lurline*) before being sold to Chandris (to rejoin *Lurline* which was now the *Ellenis*) in 1970. Initially used in the UK–Australia emigrant trade, she cruised part of the season out of the US from 1975, and almost permanently from 1981. Laid up in 1995, she sank off South Africa on 21 October 2000 whilst being towed to the breakers.

Victoria: Mentioned earlier as a conversion for Icres Lines from the *Dunnottar Castle*, *Victoria* became a Chandris vessel in 1975 under the name of *The Victoria*. In Chandris's service she worked in both the Mediterranean and Scandinavia for the European market, and out of San Juan (Puerto Rico) for the US market.

Chandris acquired the *Galileo Galilei* from the Italians in 1983, and it was this ship that led to the formation of Celebrity Cruises, an operation covered later in this book.

In this section we have focussed quite strongly on Chandris because of the role that the company played in the development of the current American market, with important links to Celebrity Cruises and to Royal Caribbean. The company is also important for the number of ex-US liners it purchased and rejuvenated.

A partnership called Chandris-Fantasy Cruises started in the early 1980s, and was later divided into two separate arms of the Chandris Group: Fantasy-Cruises and then the more up-market North American-oriented Celebrity Cruises. Soon after, in 1990, Celebrity Cruises commissioned its first brand new, purpose-built ships, the sisters *Horizon* and *Zenith*.

By the 1980s there was a plethora of companies operating in the North American market, some old, some European such as Cunard and Costa that expanded rapidly into the burgeoning sector, and some new entrants who were to become, eventually, the major players.

Enter Miami

Miami was just a small cruise port in the early 1960s. Five old cruise ships – *Bahama Star*, *Yarmouth*, *Yarmouth Castle* (sadly burnt out in 1965), *Evangeline* and *Florida* – were based there, all sailing around 5p.m. on a Friday for the Bahamas and the Caribbean. This was all to change, however, and with the development of Dodge Island as one of the world's greatest cruise ports, Miami was to become the cruising hub of North America. Eastern Cruise Lines were mentioned earlier in this book, and the company was an important part of the early Miami cruising scene. Built as a Swedish car ferry in the early 1950s, *Patricia,* when not on the North Sea, was involved in early post-war cruising out of New York. Sold in 1957 to Hamburg America as the cruise ship *Ariadne*, she was then sold in 1961 to Eastern Cruise Lines who used her under the same name on the Miami–Bahamas cruise ferry run. She was later chartered by Eastern to Freeport Cruise Lines under the name *Freeport 11* on a similar service.

The Peninsular and Occidental Steamship Line (not to be confused with the famous British company P&O, which started life as the Peninsular & Oriental Steamship Company) had one vessel, the *Florida* (see above), another early Miami cruise ship. She was later replaced by the *Miami* (ex-*Jerusalem*).

However, the transformation of Miami into the huge cruise centre that it is today can be laid at the feet of two men: Ted Arison and Knut Kloster. In 1966, Ted Arison (later to be the founder of Carnival Cruises and the Carnival Group) and the Norwegian shipping company of Kloster Reederei, formed a partnership to offer Caribbean cruises from Miami, Florida. Kloster provided *Sunward*, which had been built as a passenger ferry designed for the UK–Spain service, and Arison marketed the cruise package in North America.

In her original role, *Sunward* had been a victim firstly of the UK currency restrictions that had caused a drop in demand for foreign holidays, and secondly, Spain's intransigence over her claims of sovereignty over Gibraltar. The new company was given the name of Norwegian Caribbean Line, a name changed to Norwegian Cruise Line in 1987.

Disagreements between Knut Kloster and Arison led to a parting of ways in 1972, and Arison set up Carnival Cruises now, as Carnival Group, the biggest cruise operator not just in North America but globally. Carnival began in 1972 with just one ship, the 18,261-GRT *Mardi Gras*, which had started life as *Empress of Canada*. From that one ship, which actually ran aground on its maiden voyage for Carnival, has grown the mighty Carnival Empire.

Following the success of NCL, two other major Scandinavian companies entered the Caribbean market – Royal Caribbean Cruise Line (still operating today as Royal Caribbean International) and Royal Viking Line (first acquired by Kloster in 1984 and then by Cunard in 1994 and, eventually, in 1998, by Carnival as part of the take over of Cunard in that year). The Scandinavian influence has remained strong within the North American cruise marketplace ever since.

Sunward was followed by a distinctive design of vessels, *Starward* (1968), *Skyward* (1969) and *Southward* (1971), all between 12 and 17,000 GRT and all designed for 7-day Caribbean cruises out of Miami.

Fred Olsen's *Boudicca* was originally *Royal Viking Sky* and, as such, brought new standards to the American cruise market.

From 1969 to 1971 Royal Caribbean Cruise Line (RCCL), now Royal Caribbean International (RCI), introduced three vessels, *Song of Norway*, *Nordic Prince* and *Sun Viking*, each of about 18,000 GRT and each designed for 700–800 guests. They featured distinctive lounges positioned halfway up their funnels. *Song of Norway* and *Nordic Prince* were later lengthened to accommodate some 1,200 passengers.

Royal Viking Line followed suit with their trio of ships, albeit to a slightly different philosophy. *Royal Viking Star* (1971), *Royal Viking Sky* (1972) and *Royal Viking Sea* (1973) were bigger, at 21,800 GRT, but carried only 550-560 passengers. They too were later lengthened to become 28,000+ GRT and capacity increased to 812. (In their later lives, many of these North American market ships were sold to new entrants into the cruise industry, and a number of them operated in the UK market for new owners.) The rest of the RCI story is told later.

North America led the growth in the cruise industry in the 1970s and 1980s, with new companies being formed each year, as well as ones leaving the market or being bought up.

DODGE ISLAND

Compared to New York, Miami offered a significant geographical advantage for cruises to the Caribbean, and an increasing number of operators capitalised on this, re-locating their base ports from New York, the result being that in a relatively short time more land was needed to expand the port operation. On 5 April 1960, the Dade County Board of Commissioners approved Resolution No.4830, 'Joint Resolution Providing for Construction of Modern Seaport Facilities at Dodge Island Site'. The City of Miami approved this resolution the following day, and work soon began on the construction of a new port on Dodge Island.

This was achieved by expanding the island itself and then linking it by bridges to other islands in the general vicinity. As soon as the new seawalls, transit shed A, administration building and a new vehicle and railroad bridge were complete, operations were transferred from the mainland port to the new Dodge Island facility. Through the years thereafter, additional reclamation enlarged the islands of

Celebrity *Century* at Key West.

Adventure of the Seas at St Lucia.

Melody towards the end of her career, seen entering Brazillian waters.

Lummus and Sams, along with the filling of the north, south and National Oceanic and Atmospheric Administration slips, creating the new port which stands today on land that is almost completely man-made.

At the time of writing, it is fair to say that the Port of Miami is the cruise capital of the world and the cargo gateway of the Americas. It has retained its status as the number one cruise/guest port in the world for well over two decades, accommodating the largest cruise ships in the world and the operations of major cruise lines such as Carnival, Royal Caribbean and Norwegian Cruise Line.

By the end of the twentieth century, Jacksonville, Port Everglades and Fort Lauderdale had also become major base ports in Florida, reflecting the huge increase in Caribbean cruising. The ports of the Gulf of Mexico have also expanded into the cruise market, providing extra cruising opportunities for those in the Mid-West.

CRUISE AMERICA GOES GLOBAL

When the Greek-flagged *Golden Odyssey* of Royal Cruise Lines entered service in 1974, it was no coincidence that her 460-guest capacity was very similar to that of the Boeing 747 which had been introduced in 1969. Fly-cruising was becoming more and more popular, and Americans and Canadians no longer had to confine themselves to cruising out of US and Canadian ports. Southampton and Dover in the UK, Barcelona in Spain, Civitavecchia (the port for Rome), Athens and Istanbul rapidly became the base ports for US market ships undertaking a Mediterranean season. Today, US market ships are based across the globe from Shanghai to Buenos Aires, offering fly-cruises for American cruise passengers.

FAMILY/FUN CRUISES

Although cruising was still seen as being stuffy and only for the better off, changes were afoot, though there are still traditional-style cruises which will be considered later. The North American market has, however, led the way in fun-filled, family cruising. From its inception in 1972, Carnival Cruises marketed itself to a younger set and provided plenty of fun and activities, especially for children.

In 1974, Premier Cruise Line was formed by Bruce Nierenberg and Bjornar Hermansen, two men with links to the Greyhound bus company. The company's first ship was the Costa liner *Federico C.*, which was refitted and given a distinctive red hull. She was renamed *Royale*, but was often described as *StarShip Royale*, and operated 3-day and 4-day Bahamas trips out of Port Canaveral. The second ship, acquired in 1986, was the Home Lines' flagship *Oceanic*, renamed *StarShip Oceanic*. (She became the *Peaceboat* in 2009.) Subsequent purchases in 1988 were the Home Lines' *Atlantic*, sold by Holland America when Home Lines were acquired, and *Sun Princess (ex-Spirit of London)* of Princess Cruises. These became *StarShip Atlantic* and *StarShip Majestic*. *StarShip Royale* was sold to Dolphin Cruise Line as *SeaBreeze* in the same year when these newer ships arrived.

During the 1980s, the company was earning in excess of $20 million annually on a gross revenue of $100 million. Nierenberg and Hermansen sold their shares back to Greyhound. *SeaBreeze* rejoined Premier Cruises' fleet when that company amalgamated with Dolphin. Premier became the official Disney cruise line, and marketed cruises as part of a package including visits to the Disney theme parks in Florida, although this connection was severed when Disney created its own cruise line.

StarShip Majestic was sold to CTC Cruise Lines in 1994, becoming their *Southern Cross*, and *StarShip Atlantic* was sold to MSC Cruises to become their *Melody*. This left only *StarShip Oceanic* in the fleet before the amalgamation with Dolphin and Seawind to form the new Premier Cruises.

The new Premier Cruises fleet was an amalgamation of Dolphin Cruise Line; *SeaBreeze*, *OceanBreeze* and *IslandBreeze*. The original Premier Cruise Line's *Oceanic* was marketed as the 'Big Red Boat'. The former Dutch liner *Rotterdam* was then acquired to become the *Rembrandt*. For a time, a new blue colour scheme was applied to all vessels except *Oceanic*. In an attempt to gain a family market, ships of the fleet later became *Big Red Boat II*, *III*, *IV* etc. The final addition to the fleet was the vessel which became the *Big Red Boat II*, ex-*Eugenio Costa*.

Sadly, Premier Cruises collapsed in September 2000, but by the time of its collapse the needs of families were well catered for by the American cruise market, with Carnival, Royal Caribbean and Norwegian Cruise Line all equipping their ships with family-style activities. Rock Climbing, wave pools and even ice skating were on offer on board. These newer vessels were designed to be floating resorts and could compete not only within the cruise industry, but also with land-based vacations – and they appealed to families.

Launched in December 1993, American Family Cruises, a joint venture between Costa and Bruce Nierenburg (a founder of Premier Cruises), was specifically aimed at young American families with children. *Costa Riviera* was renamed *American Adventure* for this service. However, the venture was unsuccessful and the ship sailed for Genoa in September 1994 where she was converted back to the *Costa Riviera*. Citing a lack of consistent business, the plans for a second vessel (*Eugenio Costa* to be renamed *American Pioneer*) were abandoned.

DISNEY CRUISE LINE

In 1998 and 1999 respectively, Disney introduced the 83,000 GRT+ *Disney Magic* and *Disney Wonder*, perhaps the ultimate in child-centred cruising, although both ships do have adult-only areas. Disney also has its own private island, Castaway Cay, and has announced two new, much bigger 128,000 GRT vessels for 2011 and 2012, *Disney Dream* and *Disney Fantasy*, both from the Myer Weft yard in Germany.

Disney were one of the first companies to introduce yellow lifeboats, which neatly fitted their corporate image, and the vessels abound with Disney features from a Goofy painting on the stern to Mickey's ears on the funnels.

The Church of Scientology also has its own cruise ship (it has been at the centre of a number of asbestos scares in recent years). Technically owned by Majestic Cruises on behalf of the church, *Freewinds* was built as the *Boheme* and spent her early years chartered to Commodore Cruises.

Opposite, clockwise from top left

Disney Magic may present a strange appearance, but she is how a child would draw a ship.

The bow decoration of *Disney Magic*.

Goofy painting the stern of *Disney Magic*.

Mickey's ears adorn the smokestack of *Disney Magic*.

Carnival Paradise departs Ensenada, Mexico, after a cabotage stop..

CHAPTER FIVE

The Onset of the Mega-Ships

THE MASSIVE GROWTH IN THE SIZE OF NORTH AMERICAN CRUISE SHIPS

Douglas R. Burgess jr wrote:

For the price of admission the passenger was removed from the reality of everyday existence and placed within a cosseted and quite unworldly atmosphere. Neither in one country nor another, neither on land nor in the air, the 6-day voyage was akin to being suspended in a netherworld – familiar yet somehow unreal – where all the distractions of normal life were replaced with forced inactivity, self indulgence and sloth.

Douglas R. Burgess jr, *Seize the Trident*, McGraw Hill, 2005.

Burgess could have describing a modern cruise ship, but he was not. He was referring to the trans-Atlantic liners of the early twentieth century, *Lusitania, Mauretania, Olympic, Titanic* and others which were huge for their day.

In the 1970s and early 1980s, North American market cruise ships were typically between 17,000 and 30,000 GRT, as larger ships such as *Queen Mary* and *Queen Elizabeth* had not been very successful in the cruising role. But in 1977, the Kloster Company (now operating as Norwegian Cruise Line) acquired the 66,000 GRT *France,* idle since 1974, and renamed her *Norway.* The addition of two new decks increased her size to 76,000 GRT, but despite this she was successful, although she had to tender at the vast majority of Caribbean ports. Her success led the way towards bigger and bigger ships. Soon, 80,000 GRT was reached, and in 1996, 100,000 GRT was passed when the 101,353 GRT *Carnival Destiny* entered service.

Too big for the Panama Canal, *Carnival Destiny* was soon followed by 100,000+ GRT vessels from Princess and Royal Caribbean. 150,000 GRT was reached with the *Queen Mary 2* of Cunard in 2003, but this was eclipsed in 2006 by the 158,000 GRT *Freedom of the Seas* and her sisters from Royal Caribbean, whose Project Genesis ships, the first of which, *Oasis of the Seas* (late 2009), is an enormous 220,000 GRT.

These are family-friendly floating resorts, complete with ice rinks, rock climbing walls, wave pools, putting courses and huge shopping malls – a far cry from the 16,000 GRT vessels which started the current boom. In contrast, there has also been a growth in the more traditional style of cruising within the North American market. Premium brands such as Oceania Cruises, Silverseas, Crystal and Regent (previously Radisson Seven Seas Cruises) operate smaller vessels on a more traditional basis, often aiming for a country house ambience, rather than striving for the creation of a floating resort. Carnival began the trend by building a series of similar ships in batches of up to six, and this has been continued by Renaissance and Royal Caribbean.

Testament to the importance of families to North American cruising is the fact that Disney, most famous of organisations for children of all ages, has well and truly established itself in the cruise business, as has been said. On a design note, the current Disney ships have two funnels, just like the ships a child would draw – clever marketing!

Resort-style mega ships are renowned for their excellent facilities for children.

The trends are interesting. Firstly, the growth in the North American market can be seen clearly. The total tonnage has tripled from just over 3 million, in 1994, to 10.5 million in 2010, but the number of vessels has only increased by 48 (44%). Many older ships have been withdrawn to be replaced by newer ones, but the staggering statistic is the increase in size of many of the newer vessels. The average tonnage of a North American cruise ship has increased from just under 30,000 GRT, to nearly 67,000 GRT – a doubling of the average in just fourteen years.

Such increases are not new. Between 1897 and 1907, the size of the largest liner on the North Atlantic doubled, and between 1906 and 1912 it almost tripled (the *Kronprizessin Cecile* of 1906 was 19, 360 GRT, whilst the *Imperator* of 1913 was 52,117 GRT).

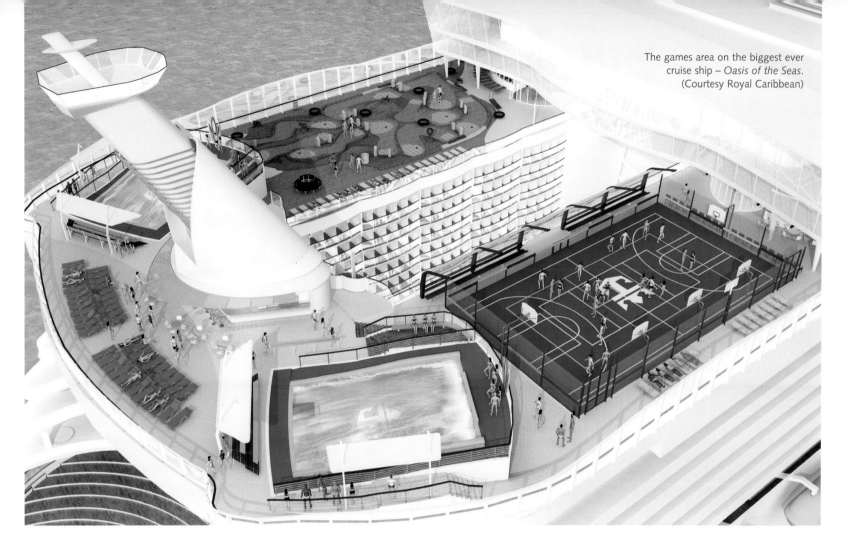

The games area on the biggest ever cruise ship – *Oasis of the Seas*. (Courtesy Royal Caribbean)

	1994	1994	1999	1999	2005	2005	2010	2010
GRT	Total GRT	No. of vessels	Total GRT	No. of vessels	Total GRT	No. of vessels	Total GRT	No. of vessels
<19K	380,545	41	500,997	29	136,907	41	150,037	35
19-49K	1,593,081	49	1,386,447	40	533,279	16	634,848	20
50-74K	1,084,982	17	1,966,069	30	1,967,024	31	1,643,938	25
75-99K	76,049	1	936,751	12	2,626,832	31	3,505,190	41
100-149K	0	0	311,654	4	2,053,350	18	3,314,304	28
150-199K	0	0	0	0	0	0	763,221	5
200K+	0	0	0	0	0	0	440,000	2
Total GRT	3,134,657	108	5,101,918	115	7,317,329	137	10,451,538	156
Average	29,025		44,365		53,412		66,997	

Figure 5: North American Market Growth In Size and Number of Vessels 1994–2010

The table also shows how the number of medium-sized ships (20–49,000 GRT) has diminished by more than half since 1994, although there is evidence of a reversal of this trends, perhaps due to the increasing popularity of the country club style of cruising which is best suited to this size of vessel – large enough to provide a variety of facilities, but small enough to be intimate.

How do these mega ships in the North American market compare to their predecessors? A comparison of the original Love Boats®, the 20,000 GRT *Pacific Princess* (ex-*Sea Venture*) and *Island Princess* (ex-*Island Venture*) of 1972, and the current 92,000 GRT *Island Princess* of 2003, proves interesting. A further comparison with the largest cruise liner, the 220,000 GRT *Oasis of the Seas* of 2009 is even more so.

Broadway-style theatres are now the norm on larger cruise ships. (Courtesy Royal Caribbean)

	Pacific Princess (1972)	*Island Princess* (2003)	*Oasis of the Seas* (2009)
GRT	20,000	92,000	225,282
Length in Feet	553	950	1187
Beam	81	106	208
Max. No. of Guests	720	2,590	5,400
Crew	300	895	2,115
Balcony Rooms	0	720	1,956 *
Restaurants	1	2	1
Alt. Restaurants/ Food Outlets	1	9	15
Bars			
Swimming pools		3 + splash pool	(See detailed breakdown below)
Whirlpools		5	
Theatre	0	1	
Show lounge	2	2	
Cinema	1	1 outdoor	
Casino	1 small + slots	1 large	
Golf course	0	9 hole putting + simulator	
Spas	1 beauty shop	2	
Library	1 small	1	
Shopping gallery	1 small shop	1	
Art Gallery	0	1	
Wedding chapel	0	1	

Island Princess, whilst quite large, still follows a fairly traditional format. She is a very elegant vessel inside and has a quite striking and modern profile. With her alternative restaurants and even a putting course, she provides a large variety of activities for her guests. She is a natural progression from her 1972 predecessor.

OASIS OF THE SEAS

Oasis of the Seas, however, is an altogether different type of cruise product. We are grateful to Royal Caribbean for providing the information and details below. As the ship may serve as the prototype not only of new vessels, but also of a new genre of cruising, we have included as much information about her as possible.

Commentators have often referred to the mega-ships as being more like floating resorts than ships. In the *Oasis of the Seas* class, this statement has become a reality. The idea of the ship itself as the destination is not new: a cruise on the *QE2*, for example, was an aspiration for many because of the image conjured up by the name, social cachet and reputation of the ship itself – her destinations were often of secondary importance.

Oasis of the Seas is a destination in herself, and lives up to the Royal Caribbean slogan of 'The Nation of Why Not'. The ship's official statistics supplied by Royal Caribbean are:

225,282 GRT
    1,187ft (360m) long
    208ft (65m) wide
    30ft (9.1m) draft
    22.6 knots cruising speed
    16 passenger decks
    24 passenger elevators
    4 bow thrusters with 7,500hp each

5,400 guests (double occupancy)
6,296 guests (total)
2,165 crew (from over 65 countries)

STATEROOMS:

Total: 2,706
       Balcony: 1,956
       Outside: 254
       Interior: 496
Staterooms with additional berths: 683
Wheelchair accessible staterooms: 46

Traditionally, ships have been divided up into decks. *Oasis of the Seas* is divided into seven neighbourhoods:

CENTRAL PARK

The Central Park neighbourhood is the first ever living park at sea. Revolutionary in design, it is open to the sky in the very centre of the ship and spans more than a football field in length. It features lush, tropical grounds planted with 12,175 plants, 62 vine plants, 56 trees and bamboo (some over 24ft (7.3m) in height). It is an upscale, exquisite, public gathering place, featuring serene pathways, seasonal flower gardens and canopy trees, and is designed to provide guests with many more choices in an outdoor space that is truly unique. Combining a large number of retail, entertainment and dining venues, with quiet nooks for reading and relaxing, Central Park is one of the ship's most groundbreaking spaces. The neighbourhood includes:

150 Central Park, the most exclusive dining venue on the ship provides an intimate dining experience. Managed by Keriann Von Raesfeld, an award-winning, internationally acclaimed chef who, at twenty-three years old, holds the title of Best Young Cook in the World.
A central Piazza, forming the ship's town square, which at night becomes a gathering space for alfresco dining and entertainment, including concerts, street performances and strolling musicians and players.
Dazzles, spanning three decks with expansive floor-to-ceiling windows, offers breathtaking views of the Boardwalk below. Located near Central Park, this dance lounge offers a variety of musical experiences ranging from 1940s big band, to disco, to ballroom evenings. During the day, Dazzles is open for guests to enjoy the view of the bustling activity on the Boardwalk over a drink, or to learn a new dance move with a professional dance instructor.
Accommodation includes 324 inward-facing balcony staterooms with a view of Central Park.
3 retail outlets, including:
       Art Actually @Parkside Gallery

       Coach – the brand's largest store at sea
       Picture This – portrait studio
6 restaurants/bars:
       150 Central Park
       Chops Grille
       Giovanni's Table
       Park Café
       Vintages
       Trellis Bar

BOARDWALK

Boardwalk has its inspiration on both sides of the Atlantic. It combines the features of the seaside piers that dot the coast of England and the nostalgic boardwalks of yesteryear such as Coney Island. Boardwalk is very much an area that families can enjoy. Signature elements of the Boardwalk include:

AquaTheater is a remarkable outdoor venue at the stern of *Oasis of the Seas*, with a backdrop of the ocean across the horizon. AquaTheater is an amphitheatre-style space celebrating water, with a full spectrum of day and night options, serving as a pool and an ocean front theatre with water and light shows by day, and professional aquatic acrobatic and synchronized swimming performances by night. The first of its kind and the most technologically advanced area of the ship.

Sumptuous loft living on *Oasis of the Seas*. (Courtesy Royal Caribbean)

It could be a mall anywhere in the US, but it is actually on *Oasis of the Seas*. (Courtesy Royal Caribbean)

The Carousel is one of a kind. It is the only carousel at sea. Handcrafted from poplar wood, the full-sized, traditional carousel features 18 figures suspended from stainless steel poles showcasing a time-honoured menagerie of animals such as zebras, giraffes and lions, alongside a variety of hand-painted horses including a princess horse and a crowned frog prince

Rock-climbing Walls: 2 signature rock-climbing walls flank the AquaTheater, providing a more unique experience with multiple climbing routes. Each rock wall will measure 43ft tall.

Accommodation in this neighbourhood include 6 AquaTheater suites, 221 Boardwalk-view balcony staterooms, and 8 Boardwalk-view window staterooms.

5 shops including:

> Star Pier – teen retail
>
> Carousel Cart
>
> Pinwheels – children's retail
>
> Candy Beach – specialty candy store
>
> Smile – novelty photo shop
>
> Pets at Sea

5 restaurants/bars:

> Ice-Cream Parlour
>
> Johnny Rockets
>
> Seafood Shack
>
> The Boardwalk Bar
>
> Boardwalk Donut Shop

ROYAL PROMENADE

Developed from the signature Royal Promenade featured on the Royal Caribbean Voyager and Freedom-class ships, the new design found on *Oasis of the Seas* allows guests to have a physical connection with the neighbourhood above – Central Park – as natural light cascades down from the sky. Giant glass-arched skylights, the crystal canopies, form a sculptured roof that look up into Central Park and the sky beyond. Included are:

The Rising Tide Bar – the world's first moving bar at sea – is an engineering feat that spans three decks and allow cruisers to enjoy a cocktail as they slowly move between Central Park on deck eight and the Royal Promenade on deck five.

The Mezzanine: Located towards the aft of the Royal Promenade, a mezzanine level provides sweeping views of the Promenade and features the cruise line's Schooner Bar and Adventures with Royal Caribbean International – the location of the future cruise sales desk.

Diamond Club: The forward mezzanine features the Diamond Club, the line's loyalty member club.

Accommodation includes 18 promenade view Staterooms.

7 retail outlets including:

> Focus – photo shop and gallery

The biggest – *Oasis of the Seas*.
(Courtesy Royal Caribbean)

Chops Grill on *Oasis of the Seas*.
(Courtesy Royal Caribbean)

Regalia – fine jewellery and gifts

Solera – perfume and cosmetic shop

The Shop – logo and souvenir shop

Port Merchants – liquors and sundries

Prince & Greene – boutique-style fashions

Willow – accessories shop

Nine restaurants/bars:

Sorrento's Pizzeria

Mondo Café

Café Promenade – signature café

Schooner Bar

On Air Club – Karaoke bar

Boleros – Latin dance club

Rising Tide

Globe and Atlas Pub

Champagne Bar

Pool And Sports Zone

Stretching the length of the ship, the Pool and Sports Zone features 4 unique types of pools, and 2 FlowRider surf simulators – each larger than the single FlowRider introduced on the line's Freedom-class ships – plus amazing views of Boardwalk and Central Park below.

Zip-Line: A thrilling new feature, the first zip-line at sea takes guests on a exhilarating ride across an open-air atrium suspended nine decks high above Boardwalk – a distance of more than 82ft (25m).

Beach Pool: The first beach pool at sea has a sloped entry where guests are able to wade into the water, or relax in colourful beach chairs under an umbrella as the water rolls gently beneath. Two whirlpools flank either side of the 'beach' for guests who prefer warmer waters.

Main Pool: The Main Pool with two side-by-side whirlpools.

The H2O Zone, marked by a giant octopus with its slides and water-spraying tentacles, flanked by fellow water-spouting ocean creatures. Separate wading and current pools, as well as a dedicated infant and toddler pool, are set in the interactive aquatic playground and surrounded by adult and child-sized lounge chairs.

The Sports Pool, where afternoon water team sports include basketball, badminton and water polo, while morning hours will be dedicated to lap swimming.

Solarium: Boasting a redefined layout, the adults-only Solarium features a two-deck high, glass-panelled enclave designed with seating on various 'islands' surrounded by water, providing guests with the sensation of floating on air. The open-air Solarium has a swimming pool, 2 serene whirlpools, and 4 cantilevered whirlpools suspended 136ft above the ocean.

The Solarium Bistro offers healthy casual fare during the day, and becomes a romantic and intimate setting for specialty dining and dancing under the stars

in the evenings. It is also the perfect venue for a unique late-night dance-club experience – Club 20 – made popular on the line's Freedom-class ships.

The Sports Deck also includes 2 of the popular FlowRider surf simulators, flanking either side of the elevated back deck, a 9-hole miniature golf course, Oasis Dunes and a Sports Court for games of basketball, volleyball and soccer.

Additional features of the Pool and Sports Zone:

2 retail outlets including:

Sea Trek

Breeze

9 restaurants/bars:

Wipe Out Café

Windjammer Café

Izumi – Asian Cafe

Solarium Bistro

Wipe Out Bar

Pool Bar

Sand Bar

Sky Bar

Mast Bar

Vitality At Sea Spa And Fitness Center

The Vitality at Sea Spa and Fitness neighbourhood provides various amenities that support healthy lifestyles and cater to complete body wellness. Here, guests can soothe mind, body and soul through the most advanced spa and anti-aging therapies, the latest fitness equipment and healthy dining options.

Additional features of the Vitality at Sea Spa and Fitness Centre:

Vitality Cafe

Spa Retail

Entertainment Place

Entertainment Place is the life of the ship after dark. This contemporary nightclub district provides after-dark spaces in more intimate venues, delivering a variety of entertainment each night and providing guests the opportunity to customise their evening experiences.

Inspired by prohibition-era Chicago, Jazz on 4.

Comedy Live, the comedy club

Blaze, where guests can dance the night away to pulsating music in a hip and trendy atmosphere.

Additional features of Entertainment Place:

Casino Royale

Opal Theatre

Museum of Gaming

Inside balcony cabins overlooking
Central park on *Oasis of the Seas*.
(Courtesy Royal Caribbean)

City Centre, on *Oasis of the Seas*.
(Courtesy Royal Caribbean)

YOUTH ZONE

A haven for children and teens, this home to the award-winning Adventure Ocean Youth Program features a wealth of child and teen-friendly adventures. The Youth Zone covers an area of more than 28,700 sq ft:

Kids Avenue, the central boulevard in Youth Zone, guides children through the dedicated Adventure Ocean spaces and various themed play areas.
Royal Babies and Tots is the cruise line's first nursery for infants and toddlers (6 months or older).
Oasis of the Seas also introduces new common play/learning areas, including the Workshop, where families can learn scrapbooking skills or create personalised jewellery; Imagination Studio where children can explore the world of colour and imagination through Adventure Art by Crayola; a fully equipped lab for Adventure Science Lab, where Einsteins-in-the-making can expand their knowledge; Play, a circular area where children can rollick and participate in a variety of sports and games; and Adventure Ocean Theatre, the first ever children's theatre at sea.
Adventure Ocean program age groups, where each has its own dedicated space: Royal Babies and Tots, ages 6 months to 2 years; Aquanauts, ages 3 to 5; Explorers, ages 6 to 8; and Voyagers, ages 9 to 11.
Long-time favourite Royal Caribbean teen-only spaces, Fuel disco and The Living Room are also provided aboard Oasis of the Seas.
Kids Arcade
Challengers Arcade

Accommodation ranges from inside staterooms through to suites, including New York-style loft apartments.

Given the facilities on board the Oasis of the Seas, it remains to be seen whether more people decide to remain at sea on a more permanent basis in the future. The ship is revolutionary – it is a floating resort and is truly remarkable.

On the subject of residing on ships, it is worth noting that, in 2001, eighty-two-year-old Beatrice Muller became the sole resident on the QE2. The American widow paid £3,440 a month for her cabin, but reckons it was a bargain compared with the cost of a residential care home. She moved into Cabin 4068 on the fourth deck of the Cunard ship 9 months after her husband died on board as the ship sailed out of Bombay. The couple, from Bound Brook, New Jersey, near New York, fell in love with the QE2 when they took a world cruise in 1995 and had planned to spend a year on board together. After the death of her husband, her son persuaded Mrs Muller to take one last cruise, and she decided to make a permanent home on the 67,000-GRT vessel. Mrs Muller is reported to have funded her lifestyle by selling two of her three homes.

Ships such as Oasis of the Seas may herald a new type of cruising. One where the itinerary is less important, with the ship itself being the destination. There will, we believe, always be a market for the more traditional cruise product, as

exemplified by Island Princess and for those seeking the more social aspects of cruising in the smaller country club-style ships which are covered below. Huge mega-ships will suit most, offering as they do those facilities more usually found in large land-based resorts and theme parks, but to some they may lack that special social interface: if you are one of 500 guests it is easy to socialise, but this may be harder to achieve when you are one of 6,000!

SIZE ISN'T EVERYTHING

There remain a reasonable number of small ships of less than 20,000 GRT. Many of these, catering to the luxury end of the market, are operated by Seabourn or SeaDream Yacht Club, or the smaller expedition operators such as:

Adventure Cruise Lines (California, Washington State, Hawaii, Alaska)
  Pacific Monarch

American Safari Cruises (California, Washington State, Mexico, Alaska)
  Safari Explorer

Canadian Sailing Expeditions (Canada, Caribbean)
  Caledonia

Classic Cruises of Newport (New England, Virgin Islands)
  Arabella

Cruise North Expeditions (Canada, Greenland)
  Lyubov Orlova (part of the Quark Expeditions of the US Fleet owned by TUI in Germany)

St Lawrence Cruise Lines (St Lawrence and Ottawa Rivers)
  Canadian Empress

Cruise West (Alaska, Central America, Mexico, West Coast, South Pacific)
  Pacific Explorer, Spirit of '98, Spirit of Alaska, Spirit of Columbia, Spirit of Discovery, Spirit of Endeavour, Spirit of Glacier Bay, Spirit of Oceanus, Spirit of Yorktown

With ships whose size range between 100 to 15,000 GRT, these operators show that there are opportunities for companies that wish to establish a niche far removed from that of the mega-ships. The sailing vessels that offer luxury cruises, such as Royal Clipper and Windstar, are larger, but still fall into the small ship category.

CHAPTER SIX

Disasters —
Fortunately Few and Far Between

SINKINGS AND PIRATES

The worst ever cruise disaster did not involve North American guests. On 31 August 1986, the *Admiral Nakimov*, built in 1925 as the German vessel *Berlin*, collided with a cargo vessel and sank in the Black Sea, 8 miles from Novorossysk. 836 people were rescued, but 423 lives were lost.

The second worst loss of life involving cruise-ship guests was in the US market, but did not occur at sea. On Sunday 27 March 1977 a bomb – which caused no loss of life – damaged the passenger terminal at Las Palmas Airport in the Canary Islands. As a result, flights were diverted to Los Rodeos Airport on neighbouring Tenerife. Amongst the flights diverted was a KLM Boeing 747 bound for Las Palmas on a charter holiday flight from Amsterdam, and a Pan American 747 operating a charter for Royal Cruise Line. 364 passengers, most of them of retirement age, had boarded at Los Angeles for the first stage of a charter flight to Gran Canaria. They were due to join the line's *Golden Odyssey* for a 12-day Mediterranean cruise. Departing LAX late the previous afternoon, they had flown direct to John F. Kennedy Airport in New York where the aircraft was refuelled, fourteen additional passengers were boarded, and the crew changed.

When Las Palmas Airport opened, there was a need to deal with the congestion at Tenerife. The KLM flight taxied to the end of the runway in somewhat misty conditions, and the plan was for the Pan American flight to taxi part of the way along the runway and then to turn off onto a taxiway. In the mist, the turning was missed, and at the same time the KLM pilot, believing that he had permission to take off, was almost airborne when the Pan American aircraft collided with it, resulting in a massive conflagration. All 248 people on the KLM flight died, and only sixty-one out of 396 of those on the Pan American flight survived. The death toll of 583 makes it the worst air disaster ever. Although not a disaster directly involving a ship, its association made it a cruise-related disaster second only to the loss of the *Admiral Nakimov*.

It is not collisions (with other ships, rocks or even icebergs) that are the biggest danger to a cruise ship, but fire that is the paramount risk at sea – a fact that is always emphasised at guest emergency drills. Cunard's *Berengaria*, a favourite 'booze cruise' ship out of New York during prohibition (see earlier), was famous for the number of small fires on board during the later stages of her career. Modern cruise ships are inspected regularly by the US Coastguard, and have multi-layer fire protection and suppression systems. Small fires do occur, often caused by guest carelessness, especially with cigarettes, but these are normally brought under control with the minimum of disruption. However, it has not always been so, and older vessels are often the most vulnerable.

Morro Castle left Havana, Cuba, on her final voyage on 5 September 1934. On the afternoon of the 6th, as the ship steamed up the south-eastern coast of the United States, the weather began to deteriorate, and by the morning of the 7th the clouds had thickened and the winds had shifted to the east. Early in the evening, newly promoted Captain Robert Willmott had his dinner delivered to his quarters. Shortly thereafter, he complained of stomach trouble and, not long after that, died of an apparent heart attack. The command of the ship passed to the next officer in seniority, Chief Officer Warms. During the overnight hours, the winds increased as the *Morro Castle* slowly made her way up the eastern seaboard.

Shortly before 3a.m., a fire was detected in a storage locker within the first-class writing room. Within the next 30 minutes, the *Morro Castle* became engulfed in flames. Chief Officer Warms attempted to beach the ship, but the growing need to launch lifeboats and abandon ship forced him to give up this strategy. Within 20 minutes of the fire's discovery, the main electric cable burned through, plunging the ship into darkness. At about the same time, the wheelhouse lost the ability to steer the ship as vital hydraulic lines were also severed by the fire. Guests, cut off by the fire amidships, began to move toward the stern, whilst most crew members moved forward to the fo'c's'le. On the ship, no one could see anything. Guests and crew began to jump overboard, but the sea, whipped by high winds, made it extremely difficult to swim.

Only six of the ship's twelve lifeboats were launched. Although the combined capacity of these boats was 408, they carried only eighty-five people, most of whom were crew members. Many passengers died due to the lack of knowledge about the correct use the life jackets, and as they hit the water many of the life jackets knocked their wearers unconscious, leading to subsequent death by drowning, or breaking their wearers' necks on impact with the sea, killing them instantly. (According to many accounts, this also accounted for many of the deaths on *Titanic*.) Rescue ships were slow to arrive, and the seriousness of the situation was not recognised by various ships in the vicinity.

As news of the disaster spread along the coast by telephone and radio, local citizens assembled on the coastline to retrieve the dead, nurse the wounded, and try to unite families that had been scattered between different rescue boats that were landing on the New Jersey beaches. By mid-morning, the ship was totally abandoned and its hull drifted ashore, coming to a stop in shallow water off Asbury Park, New Jersey, where the fires smouldered for the next two days. In the end, 135 passengers and crew (out of a total of 549) were lost.

The ship was declared a total loss, and its charred hulk was finally towed away from the Asbury Park shoreline on 14 March 1935 to be sold for scrap. In the intervening months, during which time it was possible to wade out and physically touch the wreck, it was treated as a destination for ghoulish sightseers. In the inquiries that followed the disaster, there were criticisms of the Chief Officer's ship handling, the crew's response to the fire, and the delay in calling for assistance.

The small cruise ship, *Yarmouth Castle* (ex-*Evangeline* – see earlier), left Miami heading for Nassau on her usual cruise route on 12 November 1965, with 376 guests and 176 crewmen aboard – a total of 552 people. The ship was due to arrive in Nassau the next day. The captain on the voyage was thirty-five-year-old Byron Voutsinas, relatively young for one in such a responsible position.

Shortly before 1.00a.m. on 13 November, a mattress stored too close to a lighting circuit in a storage room (Room 610) caught fire. The room was filled with bedding and paint which fed the flames. At around 1.00a.m., a badly burned guest emerged from a stairway and collapsed on the deck. Crewmen who rushed to the man's aid found the stairwell filled with smoke and flames. Captain Voutsinas was immediately notified of the fire by the officer of the watch, and he ordered the second officer to sound the alarm on the ship's whistle, but the bridge was engulfed by flames before the alarm could be sounded. The radio room was also gutted early on.

At this point, *Yarmouth Castle* was 120 miles east of Mihpi and 60 miles north-west of Nassau. The ship's fire alarms and sprinklers did not work and panic ensued. The fire swept through the ship's superstructure at great speed, driven by the ship's ventilation system, and flames rose up stairwells fuelled by the wood panelling, wooden decks and layers of fresh paint on the bulkheads. Many guests had to break windows and squeeze through portholes to exit their burning cabins. The whole front half of the ship was quickly engulfed, causing guests and crew to flee to the sternmost areas. Several lifeboats caught fire before they could be launched.

The Finnish-registered cargo vessel, *Finnpulp*, was just ahead of *Yarmouth Castle*, heading in the same general direction. Her officers noticed on their radar that *Yarmouth Castle* had slowed significantly, and they saw the glowing flames. *Finnpulp* sent out the first Mayday call. *Bahama Star* was following *Yarmouth Castle* at about 12-miles distance. Her captain saw smoke and a red glow, and ordered the ship ahead at full speed. *Finnpulp* reached the first of *Yarmouth Castle*'s lifeboats, which was only half full with four guests and twenty crewmembers who had fled at the first alarm, among them Captain Voutsinas. The four passengers were taken aboard the freighter. The next two lifeboats contained only crew.

By this time, *Bahama Star* had arrived on the scene. The ship stopped 100yds from *Yarmouth Castle* and launched its lifeboats, which lined up against the side of the burning ship. Some people jumped into the water and climbed aboard the lifeboats. Others descended via ropes and rope ladders. *Finnpulp* lowered one of her boats which towed some lifeboats to *Bahama Star*. *Finnpulp* actually pulled alongside *Yarmouth Castle*, and passengers stepped from the burning ship onto the deck of the freighter. However, *Finnpulp* was quickly forced to retreat to a safe distance when its paint began to smoke and burn.

All survivors had been pulled aboard *Finnpulp* and *Bahama Star* by 4.00a.m., by which time *Yarmouth Castle*'s hull was glowing red. Just before 6.00a.m., *Yarmouth Castle* rolled over onto her port side and sank. Fourteen critically injured people were taken by helicopter from *Bahama Star* to Nassau. *Bahama Star* rescued 240 passengers and 133 crewmen. The *Finnpulp* rescued fifty-one passengers and forty-one crewmen. Both ships arrived in Nassau on 13 November. Eighty-seven people went down with the ship, and three of the rescued passengers later died in hospital, bringing the final death toll to ninety. Of the dead, only two were crewmembers.

In October 1980, whilst re-positioning to the Far East, Holland America's 1973-built *Prinsendam* suffered an engine room fire which spread into the guest areas of the ship. She later sank in the Gulf of Alaska. This could have been a major tragedy, but thanks to the heroics of the crew and the US Coastguard, 324 passengers and 200 crew were rescued in a dramatic operation with no casualties.

On 30 March 1979, whilst on a Caribbean cruise, *Angelina Lauro* (the former Dutch liner *Oranje* of 1939), at the time chartered to Costa, caught fire in the US Virgin Islands. St Thomas was not as busy as it is today, but it was still a major cruise port. The ship was berthed and her guests were ashore when fire broke out in her aft galley and rapidly spread forward through the restaurants and passenger accommodation. The crew did everything possible to contain the fire but were overwhelmed, and soon flames roared from her top decks. She sank in the shallow, dockside waters. She was declared to be a total loss and remained at St Thomas for some three months.

On 2 July 1979 she was refloated, and sold for scrap to Taiwanese breakers she departed under tow on 30 July. Successfully navigating the Panama Canal and heading across the Pacific, it was not immediately apparent that the fire had weakened her hull. However, on 21 September she began to take on water, which saw her slowly listing. Even though her list increased, she remained afloat for 3 days, but, by the evening of 23 September she was fully on her side. It was not until early the next morning, just before sunrise, that she sank just 20 days after her fortieth anniversary.

Built in 1913, the *Noronic* was designed for passenger and freight service on the Great Lakes. When full to capacity, she carried 600 passengers and 200 crew. One of the largest and most beautiful passenger ships in Canada at the time, she was nicknamed 'The Queen of the Lakes'. She had two sister ships, *Huronic* and *Hamonic*. The *Hamonic* burned in 1945 with the loss of one life – an ominous precedent.

On 14 September 1949, *Noronic* left Detroit on a 7-day pleasure cruise on Lake Ontario with two overnight stops in Canada before returning to Detroit. Most of her 524 passengers were Americans. The captain on the voyage was Captain William Taylor, who headed a crew of 171. On the evening of Friday 16 September, *Noronic* docked for the night in Toronto. In the early morning, a passenger noticed smoke in the aft part of the starboard alleyway on C-deck. He followed the smell of smoke to a small room off the port corridor, just forward of a ladies' restroom. He notified a crew member and, unfortunately, the crewmember opened the closet from which smoke was issuing. Once the closet was opened, the fire exploded into the hallway. It spread quickly, fuelled by the lemon-oil-polished wood panelling. Fire hoses were non-functioning and the fire spread rapidly. The passenger grabbed his family and rushed ashore.

A passenger named Church O'Neil, a bellboy and another passenger attempted to fight the blaze with fire extinguishers, but were forced to retreat almost immediately by the spreading flames. To his dismay, O'Neil found the ship's fire hoses to be out of order. Church rushed to his stateroom on D-deck and he, his wife and children quietly fled the ship. The fire spread and grew rapidly, and as rescuers arrived people were frantically jumping into the lake.

By this time, the entire ship was consumed in flames. Crew members had failed to make a sweep of the upper four decks to awaken guests, and those who did wake up did so to screams and pandemonium. Most of the ship's stairwells were on fire, and few passengers were able to reach E-deck to escape down the gangplanks. Some passengers climbed down ropes to the pier. The scene was later described as one of great panic, with people jumping from the upper decks engulfed in flames, some falling to their deaths onto the pier below. Others were trampled to death in the mad rush of terrified passengers in the corridors. Still others suffocated or were burned alive, unable to exit their cabins.

The emergency services had extinguished the blaze by 5.00a.m., and the wreckage was allowed to cool for 2 hours before the recovery of bodies began. Searchers found a gruesome scene inside the burnt-out hull. The death toll from the *Noronic* disaster was never precisely determined. Estimates range between 118 and 139. An inquiry by the Canadian government deemed it likely that a cigarette, carelessly dropped by a member of the laundry staff, had been the cause of the fire.

Other major cruise-ship fires have not involved vessels in the US market, but are included for the sake of completeness.

The *Achille Lauro* (ex-*Willem Ruys* and discussed later in connection with a hi-jacking that resulted in the death of an American guest) caught fire on 30 November 1994 and later sank in the Indian Ocean with four dead and eight injured.

On 21 May 1999, *Sun Vista* (ex-*Meridian*, ex-*Galileo*) suffered an engine room fire which spread whilst on a cruise off the coast of Malaysia. Everybody was rescued, but the evacuation was chaotic. The ship later sank.

Norwegian Dream entering port.

Sinkings not caused by fire have been relatively rare in the cruise industry. Storms may cause discomfort, but ship's masters tend to avoid them whenever possible, not because of the danger but to avoid distress to the guests. Smaller vessels, however, may be more vulnerable.

In 1995 the 234ft gambling and cruise ship, *Club Royale*, sank in the Atlantic 90 miles east of Cape Canaveral. Three crewmembers died whilst riding out Hurricane Erin. In 1998, the windjammer sailing vessel *Fantome* was trying to outrun Hurricane Mitch in the Caribbean. There were no guests onboard, but the crew of thirty died when the ship was overwhelmed and sank.

On 3 August 1991, the *Oceanos*, a small Greek cruise ship was off South Africa when she suffered an engine room explosion. The engine room flooded and the ship began to list dangerously. By good fortune, she was just within the range of South Africa's military helicopters, and all the passengers and crew were rescued. The Captain did not endear himself to anybody by being one of the first survivors into a helicopter. The real heroes were the ship's entertainers, who worked hard to assist the guests.

In the same year as the *Admiral Nakimov* disaster, 1986, the *Mikhail Lermontov*, another Russian cruise ship, sank in 100ft of water off New Zealand's South Island after hitting a reef. One crew member died, but the remainder and the guests were rescued.

In 1999, the *Norwegian Dream* of NCL was in collision with a cargo ship in the English Channel off Dover and was out of service for over two months.

Weary cruisers return to *Regatta* in Mexico.

The terrible events of 11 September 2001 had a dramatic effect on the North American cruise market. Terrorism had not previously impacted on the cruise industry, except in terms of heightened on-board security, but there was one, earlier and tragic event that did involve US citizens.

THE ACHILLE LAURO HIJACKING

Achille Lauro was completed in 1947 (laid down in 1939) as *Willem Ruys* .In 1964, she was sold to the Flotta Lauro Line, or Star Lauro (now re-branded with new, modern vessels as MSC Cruises), and renamed *Achille Lauro* (after the company's owner).

Extensively rebuilt and modernised after an August 1965 on-board explosion, *Achille Lauro* entered service in 1966 still as a traditional passenger liner, but was converted to a cruise ship in early 1972, during which time she suffered a disastrous fire. A 1975 collision with the cargo ship *Youseff* resulted in the sinking of the latter, and another on-board fire in 1981 took her out of service for a time. She was laid up in Tenerife when the Lauro Line went bankrupt in 1982. The Chandris Line took possession of her in 1985, shortly before the hijacking.

On 7 October 1985, four members of the Palestine Liberation Front (PLF) took control of the liner off Egypt as she was sailing from Alexandria to Port Said. The hijackers were surprised by a crew member and acted prematurely. Holding the passengers and crew hostage, they instructed the captain to proceed to Syria. They demanded the release of fifty of their colleagues being held in Israeli prisons. After being refused permission to dock at Tartus, the hijackers killed disabled US passenger, Leon Klinghoffer, and then threw his body overboard. The ship headed back towards Port Said, and after two days of negotiations the hijackers agreed to abandon the liner in exchange for safe conduct and were flown towards Tunisia aboard an Egyptian airliner.

On 10 October, Ronald Reagan ordered that the plane be intercepted by US navy carrier-based aircraft from the USS *Saratoga* and directed to land at a NATO airbase in Sicily. The hijackers were arrested by the Italian police, whilst the other passengers on the plane (possibly including the hijackers' leader, Abu Abbas) were allowed to continue on, despite protests by the United States. Egypt then demanded an apology from the United States for forcing the airplane off course.

The Italian Prime Minister claimed Italian territorial rights over the NATO base, and for a few hours Italian police and US special forces faced each other in a potentially hostile situation. It was the gravest diplomatic crisis between Italy and United States, but was resolved after 5 hours.

The hijackers were tried and convicted, but some later fled whilst on parole. Nobody really paid the full price for the murder. The PLO was sued for its role in the death of Leon Klinghoffer, but the $1.5 billion suit was dropped when the PLO paid an undisclosed sum to Klinghoffer's daughters. The money was used to start the Leon and Marilyn Klinghoffer Memorial Foundation, which works to combat terrorism through legal, political and educational means.

Radar and sophisticated navigation systems should render collisions almost impossible. However, the sinking of the beautiful Italian liner, *Andrea Doria*, by the *Stockholm* (now sailing as the cruise ship *Athena*) off Nantucket in 1956 with the loss of over fifty lives is often cited as the first 'Radar Assisted Collision'. If the two vessels had not spotted each other on their (by today's standards) primitive radars and taken incorrect avoiding action, they would have passed each other blissfully unaware of each other's presence. It is interesting to note that, as a direct consequence of this misuse of radar, all future deck officers (in the British Merchant Marine at least) had to qualify as radar observers before they were granted their professional Certificates of Competency. The *Andrea Doria/Stockholm* collision underscores the saying that any device is only as good as the human operating it.

Collisions between two or more ships, or with piers and the like, do occur, normally in confined channels and harbours and frequently with only minor damage. As new propulsion systems such as azipods and gas turbines have developed, there have been a number of breakdown incidents which have led to altered or curtailed itineraries, and even cancelled cruises, but new technologies have their teething problems, and the vast majority of cruises pass off without any untoward incidents.

For those who want to check up on any incidents involving cruise ships the website 'Events at Sea': http://www.cruisejunkie.com/events.html is an invaluable reference.

The ship continued in service. She was re-flagged in 1987 when the Lauro Line was taken over by the Mediterranean Shipping Company. On 30 November 1994, she caught fire off the coast of Somalia while en route to South Africa. Abandoned, the vessel sank on 2 December.

The Effects of 9/11

No cruise ships were directly affected by 9/11. The UK cruise ship *Aurora* had just left New York on a charter, with many of her guests on land tours of the US and Canada. The charter was cancelled and the guests in the US were bussed to Boston, Massachusetts, to rejoin the ship, whilst those in Canada rejoined in Halifax. Many ships remained until the situation clarified.

The US market had become very reliant on fly cruising, both within the US and from the US to foreign base ports, and following 9/11 the reluctance of many Americans to fly led to a decrease in guest loads. Premier Cruises and Renaissance Cruises were perhaps the best known casualties, both going out of business shortly afterwards.

Whilst the market has recovered, there has been an increase in home-based US cruising, with many more ports becoming base ports for North American market cruises. Miami and Fort Lauderdale have been joined by a whole series of East, West and Gulf of Mexico ports. Baltimore, Boston, Bayonne (NJ), Charleston, Galveston, Gulfport, Houston, Jacksonville, Los Angeles (both San Pedro and Long Beach), New Orleans, New York (both the older berths in Manhattan, at one time used by the liner trade, and the new Brooklyn Cruise terminal), Norfolk (VA), Philadelphia, Port Canaveral, San Diego, San Francisco, San Juan (Porto Rico) , Seattle and Tampa in the US, plus Vancouver and Montreal are now regular base ports for North American market ships.

According to the 2009 edition of the *Berlitz Guide to Cruising and Cruise Ships*, the Brooklyn Cruise Terminal and that at Vancouver had the best facilities, whilst the worst were located at Miami. In fairness to Miami, it is a very busy port, possibly the biggest in the world for cruise ships, and there are often large numbers of vessels loading at any one time. On the other side of the harbour from the mega-ship berths is Terminal J, used by smaller ships such as those owned by Oceania Cruises – a haven of calm in comparison.

Security is now much tighter, not just on US market ships but also on those of other markets, and restrictions of items that can be taken on flights have made flying all the more stressful. These measures, although considered irksome when introduced, have led to a resurgence in fly-cruising, and with it the expansion of modern cruise terminals across the world. Given that the American market is such a large percentage of the global total, it should not be surprising that many from North America use the expanded terminals at Barcelona, Malaga, Dover (England) and Leith (Scotland).

The biggest impact of 9/11 has been the increased security in the cruise industry. No longer can visitors come aboard. Baggage searches are routine, and many ports provide a security boat to patrol the immediate area around the berthed ship. Port authorities are now much stricter about immigration and security checks. It is not just the US that demands all non-citizens undertake a face-to-face check with officials, Japan does the same.

The cruise companies, especially those in the North American market, are doing all they can to ensure that cruising remains a safe option for the increasing numbers turning to this type of vacation.

Piracy

In the latter years of the twentieth century, it might have been assumed that piracy was something that was the concern of Hollywood. However, it is not *Pirates of the Caribbean* that has exercised the minds of shipping companies and the world's navies, but the pirates of Somalia. Until recently, pirate attacks off the Horn of Africa often went unreported by the media, as they usually involved assaults on small cargo ships with few western crew members.

However, in December 2005 the luxury cruise ship *Seabourn Spirit* was attacked by pirates off the coast of Somalia. Two inflatable craft, armed with rocket-propelled grenades and automatic weapons, assaulted the vessel while cruise-goers prepared to repel boarders by taking up shuffleboard sticks and empty champagne bottles. In the event, no boarding was attempted. *Seabourn Spirit* sped away (cruise ships can be very fast if necessary), while the crew used high-amplitude sound equipment to stun the pirates. The guests were mustered inside the vessel for safety. This attack did make the news.

In December 2008, *Nautica* of Oceania Cruises was attacked by pirates in the Gulf of Aden, off the coast of Somalia, en route to Oman. The ship, carrying 690 guests and 386 crew, was fired at from two small vessels during its 32-day voyage from Rome to Singapore. No one on board was hurt, and *Nautica*'s captain, Jurica Brajcic, was able to take evasive action and outrun the two boats.

'One of the skiffs did manage to close the range to 300yds and fired eight rifle shots in the direction of the vessel before trailing off,' said a statement by Oceania. 'No one aboard *Nautica* was harmed and no damage was sustained.'

This was just one week after the capture of the 330m tanker *Sirius Star*, containing 2 million barrels of oil, the largest of nearly 100 vessels to be attacked off the coast of Somalia in 2008.

In April 2009, security guards aboard the Italian market cruise ship *Melody* traded gunfire with pirates 500 miles off the coast of Somalia. On 5 March 2009, the UK cruise ship *Balmoral* was subject to a possible interception by pirates in the same area, but in the event no attack materialised.

Not surprisingly, there are now naval patrols mounted by an international fleet of warships from a number of countries including the USA, the UK, India and others, patrolling these very dangerous waters. As the Somalian economy has collapsed, piracy and the holding of crews hostage has become a routine economic activity.

CHAPTER SEVEN

The Big Players

Cruising became a mainstream vacation activity for a variety of reasons, some of which we have already touched upon. It is appropriate, therefore, to consider in greater detail some of the major operators who have played a part in its growth and development.

We begin with Admiral Cruises, the Royal Viking Line, Regency Cruises and Commodore Cruises – companies now defunct, but nonetheless ones which made a significant contribution to the industry we know today.

ADMIRAL CRUISES

The Norwegian company of Gotaas-Larsen was a tanker shipping company that bought out the Eastern Steamship Company (see earlier). In 1970, the Eastern Steamship Company was renamed Eastern Cruise Lines, reflecting the growth of its cruising business. The 6,644-GRT *Ariadne* (launched as the Swedish Lloyd North Sea's *Patricia*), became the last Eastern Steamship Company vessel before she was exchanged for the much larger 24,458-GRT Chandris ship, *Atlantis*, which later became the *Emerald Seas*.

In 1980, they acquired the *Calypso* (ex-*Southern Cross* of the UK Shaw Savill Line) for a wholly owned subsidiary, Western Cruise Lines, operating 3 and 4-day cruises out of Los Angeles as the *Azure Seas*. This ship, originally built for the UK–UK round-the-world service to Australia and New Zealand in 1954, was quite revolutionary for her day because of her engines-aft design. Gotaas-Larsen then acquired a 51 per cent interest in Sundance Cruises, which ran a single ship, *Stardancer*, in Alaska during the summer and out of Los Angeles in winter. The combined group was renamed Admiral Cruises.

1984 saw the arrival of *Emerald Seas*, which had been launched as the *General W. P. Richardson* in 1944 but had also served as American Export Lines *La Guardia*. Puchased by Chandris, she had been heavily reconstructed as a cruise ship. In 1987, Admiral ordered the *Future Seas* from French builders as the first purpose-built vessel for the US short-cruise market, though she never sailed under her intended name.

Gotaas-Larsen also had a major stake in Royal Caribbean, and the intention was to merge the companies as Royal Admiral Cruises. This development failed to materialise, and another Royal Caribbean partner bought Gotaas-Larsen. The *Stardancer* and *Future Seas* became RCCL's *Viking Serenade* and *Nordic Empress*, and the *Emerald Seas* and *Azure Seas* were both sold. Admiral ceased operations in 1992.

ROYAL VIKING LINE

Founded in 1972 by Warren Titus, Royal Viking Line catered for the top end of the market – people who could afford both the time and the money for longer cruises.

Titus's plan was for the company to have three initial identical vessels. Each vessel would be owned by one of the three major Norwegian investors, and each vessel was built by Wärtsilä in Finland. The first, *Royal Viking Star*, completed in May 1971, was owned by Bergen Line. The second, completed in July 1973, was *Royal Viking Sky*, owned by Nordenfjeldske Dampskibsselskab of Trondheim. The last of the trio, *Royal Viking Sea*, was ready in December of the same year, and her owner was A.F. Klaveness & Co., Oslo.

All three ships were some 21,500 GRT and were nearly identical in outward appearance, with tall superstructures and a single, scooped, funnel. Internally there were slight differences. The ships were intended for longer voyages, and a significant percentage of the line's clientele were wealthy retirees.

Beginning in 1980, each of the three ships was stretched by the insertion of a 93ft-long midships section, increasing their tonnage to 28,000 GRT and their guest capacity by 200 accommodated in the resultant additional cabins. The line's management believed that the stretching operation was more economical than building a fourth ship, but some of their loyal adherents felt that the modified ships had lost their intimate appeal.

Prinsendam of HAL was originally *Royal Viking Sun* and then *Seabourn Sun*.

In 1986, the line was purchased by Norwegian Caribbean Line (NCL), then part of the Kloster Group. Under Kloster ownership, Royal Viking built a fourth ship, the *Royal Viking Sun*. Constructed by Wärtsilä in Finland, she was much bigger at 39,000 GRT. The final ship built for Royal Viking was the *Royal Viking Queen*, completed in 1992. She was just 10,000 GRT, carrying only 212 passengers and sharing a general arrangement with *Seabourn Pride* and *Seabourn Spirit* of Seabourn Cruise Line, Seabourn being the latest creation of Warren Titus.

In 1990, Kloster moved the *Royal Viking Sea* to its Royal Cruise Line brand, where she took the name *Royal Odyssey*, and the *Star* to its NCL brand, where she became the *Westward*. In 1991, the *Royal Viking Sky* was transferred to NCL and renamed *Sunward*. In 1993, the *Westward* (ex-*Royal Viking Star*) became the *Star Odyssey* for Royal Cruise Line. In 1994, the Royal Viking brand and the two remaining ships (*Royal Viking Queen* and *Royal Viking Sun*) were sold to Cunard.

Royal Viking Queen operated briefly as the *Queen Odyssey* for Royal Cruise Line, then joined her sister ships at Seabourn as *Seabourn Legend*. Cunard operated the *Royal Viking Sun* with that name until 1999, when she joined her former fleet mate as the *Seabourn Sun*. (In 2002, by which time Seabourn was under Carnival ownership, she was moved to the Holland America Line as *Prinsendam*).

Today, after several more name and ownership changes, the former *Royal Viking Star* and *Royal Viking Sky* are owned and operated by Fred Olsen Cruise Lines in the UK as *Black Watch* and *Boudicca* respectively, whereas the former *Royal Viking Sea* sails for the German company, Phoenix Reisen, as *Albatros*.

REGENCY CRUISES

Founded in 1984 by Anastasios Kyriakides and William Schanz (previously president of Paquet Cruises), Regency's first ship was *Regent Sea* (ex-*Navarino*, ex-*Gripsholm* of 1957). *Regent Sea* was chartered from a well-known Greek shipowner of the day, Tony Lelakis. She entered service for Regency in November 1985, offering weekly cruises out of Jamaica.

The company expanded rapidly in the Caribbean and Alaska, using further tonnage chartered from Lelakis. Eventually the fleet consisted of seven vessels, most of which were formerly traditional ocean liners. *Regent Rainbow* (ex-*Santa Rosa*) and *Regent Jewel* (ex-*Canguro Verde* – an Italian car ferry) were rebuilt and chartered to the company. The two container ships, *Axel Johnson* and *Annie Johnson* (acquired by Costa and rebuilt as *Costa Marina* and *Costa Allegra*) were also originally destined for Regency as *Regent Sun* (to replace the existing vessel of that name), and *Regent Moon*.

Tony Lelakis took over Regency Cruises in the early 1990s. The Lelakis Group, of which Regency was only a small part, collapsed in 1995, taking Regency with it, but a number of the vessels went on to have further careers in the cruise industry.

COMMODORE CRUISE LINE

Commodore Cruise Line began operating in 1968 and was founded by Florida hoteliers Sandy Chobol and Edwin Stephan. Earlier, Chobol had operated the *Princess Leopoldina* for a season out of Florida. The first ship for Commodore was the chartered *Bohème*, one of a series of four car ferries then under construction in Finland. *Bohème* was redesigned as a cruise ship and operated 7-night trips out of Miami until 1981. *Bohème* was joined by the former Fred Olsen car ferry *Bolero*, which also ran a summer service from Portland, Maine, and Yarmouth, Nova Scotia. (*Bohème* ultimately became the Church of Scientology vessel, *Freewinds*, which operated much of the time out of Barbados and other Caribbean islands. Following major asbestos concerns she was impounded in Curacao in 2008.)

In 1983, the Greek Line's turbine liner *Olympia* joined Commodore's fleet as *Caribe I*. Commodore Cruise Line was then bought by the Scandinavian company Effjohn, which had bought the Bermuda Star Line the year before, and merged its two ships into Commodore under the names *Enchanted Isle* and *Enchanted Seas*. These ships had originally been built in 1958 as the *Argentina* and *Brasil* of Moore-McCormack, and were amongst the last US-built liners.

The three-ship fleet survived only until 1992, when *Caribe I* was sold to Regal Cruise Line as *Regal Empress*. In 1995, Effjohn sold Commodore to New York company JeMJ Financial Services. They added the ex-Soviet vessel, *Enchanted Capri*, to the fleet, sailing out of New Orleans. She was later joined by *Enchanted Sun* (ex-*Castalia*). In 1999, Commodore resurrected the brand Crown Cruise Line, one that had previously been owned by Effjohn and operated from 1987–1997.

Crown Dynasty now sails as the *Braemar* for Fred Olsen Cruise Lines and has been lengthened since the above photograph.

Crown Dynasty was re-acquired for cruises to Bermuda, but was ultimately sold to Fred Olsen Cruise Lines in 2001, re-named *Braemar*, and today operates very successfully in the UK market.

THE LOVE BOAT®, PRINCESS CRUISES AND SITMAR

Stanley B. McDonald founded Princess Cruises on the western seaboard of the USA in 1965. The company was purchased by P&O in 1974, although the US operation continued under the Princess brand. This provided P&O with an easy entry into the US market, where the P&O brand itself was less well known.

During 1974, P&O purchased *Pacific Princess* (ex-*Sea Venture*) and *Island Princess* (ex-*Island Venture*) from the defunct Flagship Cruises who had ordered the vessels in 1970. In 1977, both ships were made available to Aaron Spelling Productions and became the stars of *The Love Boat®*, a highly successful television series starring Gavin Macleod as Captain Stubbings. So successful was the series that even in the 1990s Princess were still saying, 'It's more than a cruise, it's the *Love Boat®*'.

A revamped *The Love Boat®* series was made for screening in the early years of the twenty-first century using one of the newer Princess ships. Americans became entranced with the fun, sun and romance depicted in the series, and there is no doubt that it was instrumental in raising the idea that cruising was for all within North America. The programme had the same effect in the UK when it reached British television screens.

P&O transferred their *Spirit of London* to the Princess fleet in 1974. Originally ordered by Klosters, the ship was remarkably similar in appearance to the early

NCL ships. Renamed *Sun Princess,* the 17,300-GRT vessel served Princess until 1988, and has since had a plethora of names and owners, amongst them, *Majestic, Starship Majestic, Southern Cross* (of CTC in Europe), *Flamenco* and, more recently, *New Flamenco*.

In 1979, P&O/Princess purchased the classic ex-Swedish liner, *Kungsholm,* of 1965. Rebuilt with a single funnel, she became the *Sea Princess*. Later she was transferred to the P&O fleet and was re-named *Victoria*, enjoying considerable popularity with a UK clientele.

P&O and Princess remained linked until after the merger of Carnival with P&O. Today, Princess is a separate brand and their ships no longer display the P&O logo.

The Sitmar Line was formed by Russian émigré, Alexandre Vlasov. Sitmar ships all carried a V for Vlasov on their funnels, and the Vlasov Group, now known as V Ships, is still a major owner of vessels for charter. Much involved in the Europe–Australia immigrant trade, the company switched to cruising as immigrant traffic dried up. Vlasov had acquired the Cunarders *Carinthia* and *Sylvania* in 1968. The plans for their use on line voyages to Australia did not materialise, and they remained laid up in the UK as *Fairland* and *Fairseat*. They were then converted into cruise ships, with *Fairland* being renamed *Fairwind* before entering service in 1971. These two fine conversions joined the earlier *Fairsky* and *Fairstar* in building an excellent reputation for Sitmar as a cruise line in the American market.

The *Fairsky* was sold for scrap in 1977, although a new ship of the same name was delivered in 1984. However, in 1988 Sitmar and its ships were acquired by P&O and integrated into the Princess operation. This was a major expansion for P&O, with the company becoming a major player in the North American market. Not only did P&O and its Princess operation acquire three more cruise ships, but also three ships that were building: *Sitmar FairMajesty* became *Star Princess,* and the two other vessels on the stocks ended up being launched as *Crown Princess* and *Regal Princess. Fairwind* was renamed *Dawn Princess,* and *Fairsea* became *Fair Princess. Fairstar* went to Australia for the P&O Australia cruise operation.

Princess had introduced *Royal Princess* in 1984. Of a strikingly modern design, she was the first cruise ship since the *Wilhelm Gustloff* of the Nazi era to have all outside accommodation. The Sitmar vessels and *Royal Princess* have had long careers. *Dawn Princess* and *Fair Princess* left the fleet in the mid-1990s for other markets. *Crown Princess* and *Regal Princess* went to other parts of the Carnival Group and are still hard at work, whilst *Star Princess* became, first, *Arcadia* for P&O and then *Ocean Village* (another Carnival brand). She is now in Australia. *Sky Princess* is now *Sky Wonder,* operating in the Spanish market.

Carnival Destiny, in 1996, was the first vessel of over 100,000 GRT. Too wide for the Panama Canal, she was to be the first over a series of Carnival mega-ships. Princess, not then part of the Carnival Group, responded in 1998 with the 109,000-GRT *Grand Princess* from the Fincantieri yard. Princess developed a twin track approach to new building. A series of 100,000+ GRT mega-ships were introduced: *Golden Princess* (2001), *Star Princess* (2002), *Caribbean Princess, Diamond Princess, Sapphire Princess* (2004), *Crown Princess* (2006) and *Emerald princess* (2007), and a series of slightly smaller ships ranging from 77,000–92,000

Bayou Café on board a Princess ship. (Courtesy of Princess Cruises)

The Universal Lounge on board a Princess ship. (Courtesy of Princess Cruises)

Lotus Spa on board a Princess Ship. (Courtesy of Princess Cruises)

The Wheelhouse Bar on board a Princess Ship. (Courtesy of Princess Cruises)

Sky Princess now sails
as *Sky Wonder*.

Discovery, seen here at St Lucia,
was once *Island Princess*, one of
the original Love Boats®.

Sea Princess was just one of three
American and one Italian market
ships docked at Antigua.

GRT: *Sun Princess* (1995), *Dawn Princess* (1997), *Sea Princess* (1998), *Ocean Princess* (2000), *Coral Princess* (2002) and *Island Princess* (2003).

Diamond Princess had been laid down as *Sapphire Princess*, with the original *Diamond Princess* already under construction in the Mitsubishi yard. However, a fire in October 2005 so damaged her that *Sapphire Princess* was completed first, renamed *Diamond Princess*, and once the damaged vessel had been repaired and finished, she was named *Sapphire Princess*. This enabled the company to minimise the marketing issues of a major delay to *Diamond Princess*. The 112,000-GRT *Ruby Princess* made her debut in 2008.

To further boost the UK fleet, two of the Dawn Princess-class (see later) were transferred to Southampton in 2003. *Ocean Princess* became, and still is, *Oceana*, whilst *Sea Princess* became *Adonia* – an adults-only ship. They were marketed as the new White Sisters. *Adonia* later returned to the Princess fleet, reverting to her original name, but *Oceana* remains with P&O.

In addition, Princess also acquired three of the ships of the Renaissance Cruise Line which collapsed in 2001. *Minerva 2* (ex-*R8*) was transferred to Princess in 2007 to become *Royal Princess*, whilst *R4* became *Tahitian Princess* and *R3* became *Pacific Princess*, both in 2002. In mid-2008 it was announced that *Tahitian Princess* was to be renamed *Ocean Princess* in November 2009, to reflect her global cruising role.

Given the dominance of Carnival and the Carnival Group within the global cruise industry, it seems appropriate in these pages to consider how Carnival has developed its market dominance.

WHEN THE CARNIVAL CAME TO TOWN...

The Carnival Corporation of the US is now the largest cruise company in the world. When Carnival Cruises' first vessel, *Mardi Gras* (the ex-Canadian Pacific Liner, *Empress of Canada*), left Miami on her maiden cruise in 1972, she went aground. One competing company even offered its customers a drink named 'Mardi Gras on the Rocks' – hardly an auspicious start for a new venture. However, by 2001 Carnival was not only successful, it was the market leader in the fastest growing sector of the tourism industry.

Ted Arison had been a colonel in the Israeli Army before becoming involved in the air charter business. In 1966, he joined forces with a Norwegian, Knut Kloster, whose new cruise ferry, *Sunward*, was laid up in Europe. The cruise industry was just beginning to boom in the US, and Arison suggested basing *Sunward* at the then small port of Miami. Together, Kloster and Arison formed Norwegian Caribbean Line (NCL), a company that became Norwegian Cruise Line, ultimately becoming part of Star Cruises of Thailand.

NCL was very successful, but in 1971 Arison and Kloster split up. Kloster remained with NCL and Arison acquired *Empress of Canada* from Canadian Pacific, renaming her *Mardi Gras*. Despite her inauspicious start, customers were not put off, and the new company began to flourish. *Mardi Gras* was followed in 1978 by *Festivale* (ex-*Transvaal Castle*, ex-*S.A. Vaal*). Arison grew Carnival by

two means. The first was by offering a product to a new segment of the market, the younger vacationer, the second was through the acquisition of well-known companies and brands.

By 2001, Carnival operated over 1 million GRT of cruise ships in its own name, but the Carnival Corporation as the parent company is actually much larger. Of the sixteen ships in service in 2001, eight were sisters, representing the largest bloc of sister ships built for the guest trade since the Cunard A-class vessels of the 1920s. With imaginative interior designs by Joe Farcus, each of these ships was of 70,367 GRT. Building no fewer than eight sisters was a rarity, one only repeated by Renaissance Cruises (see later).

Growth on this scale can only occur by ensuring that the product offered is exactly what the market wants. The Carnival operation is far removed from the stuffy world of dressing for dinner – a traditionalist view of cruising. Non-stop action, music and 24-hour casino operation is the order of the day on Carnival ships. In this way, the company has been able to attract, and hold, a completely new customer base. (For those wanting a more traditional ambience, there are suitable Carnival Group cruise products.) Carnival were the first company to undertake twelve-month cruising in the Caribbean, other companies relocating their ships during the hurricane season. However, statistics showed that hurricanes disrupted very few cruises, and Carnival took a gamble which paid off. Through not having to relocate ships, the company was able to build the *Carnival Destiny*, the first guest ship too wide to transit the Panama Canal. *Carnival Destiny* and her growing band of sisters (all over 101,000 GRT) have now been joined by even bigger ships from the Princess Cruises.

Star Princess became *Arcadia* and *Ocean Village*, all within the P&O and later the Carnival Group.

Coral Princess in the Caribbean.

Is it a shopping cart? – The distinctive stern of Golden Princess.

Sea Princess during her spell on the UK market as Adonia before reverting to her original name.

Emerald Princess at Istanbul.

By introducing ships that met the vacation needs of singles and younger couples and operating mainly in the Caribbean, Carnival was able to grow very rapidly. In 1984 the company launched the largest cruise line advertising campaign ever undertaken. Costing $10 million, two different 30-second advertisements were screened 133 times across the US, with apparent success, for in 1987 Carnival made its IPO (initial public offering), becoming a public corporation. The largest vessel in the Carnival brand by 2010 was the 130,000-GRT *Carnival Dream* of 2009.

Carnival Cruises took a bold step in 1998, when, responding to customer demand, they made *Carnival Paradise* a totally smoke-free ship, banning all smoking on board – a move that has been followed by other operators, but since rescinded by Carnival. In 1996 the company offered guarantees on all cruises that, if a guest was not satisfied with the product, he or she could leave the ship at the first port of call with a full refund. By 2000, Carnival had introduced cyber cafés to all the vessels in the Carnival brand fleet, further evidence of the innovation that has driven the company to the pinnacle where it stands today.

THE CARNIVAL GROUP

The Carnival brand itself appeals to young US vacationers. But of the 9.5 million people who undertook a cruise in 1999, many were neither young nor from the US. The UK is the second largest market, and the rest of Europe provides another major slice. Many of those who enjoy cruises are older in years, and the Carnival brand would not suit them. One of the best known brands catering for the more mature vacationer is Holland America Line. Its ships are all in the premium price range, and the cruises are less destination intensive than Carnival (Carnival ships typically stop at six destinations in 7 days).

Holland America has a very loyal customer base, with high repeat business rates. Holland America, like Princess Cruises (now also part of the Carnival group), has a sophisticated operation in Alaska which includes bus and rail tours, and lodges within the National Park area. In 1987, Holland America acquired a 50 per cent stake in Windstar Cruises (a company operating large sail-driven cruise ships), and completed the purchase the following year.

However, in 1988 Carnival acquired Holland America, giving it a foothold in the premier cruise market for more mature customers, and Carnival Group sold Windstar in 2007. With the take-over, very little was changed in the Holland America operation. The appearance of Holland America ships – especially the livery – remained unchanged, and they continued under their Dutch names and registry with little reference to the new ownership.

In 1991 Carnival acquired a 25 per cent stake in Seabourn Cruises (operator of a series of small, luxurious, yacht-like vessels), then in 1996 purchased a 29.6 per cent stake in the UK vacation business of Airtours Plc at a cost of $310 million. Airtours were a very new entrant into the UK cruise market, with an operation geared to the budget end of the market, linking this to their core flights-plus-hotel package holidays. The Airtours stake was soon exchanged for Airtours' holding

in Costa Cruises. Spending another $300 million in 1997, Carnival bought Costa Cruises, a major player in both the US and European standard cruise markets. Carnival also added one of the Club Med sailing cruise vessels to the Windstar fleet.

In the early years of the twentieth century, the UK Government had kept Cunard (owners of some of the greatest Atlantic liners) out of the grasp of J.P. Morgan by providing subsidies on the stipulation that Cunard remained British. This changed in 1998, when Carnival acquired the Cunard cruise operation. By 2001, the acquisitions had added thirty-three ships plus four new-builds which had a combined tonnage of 1,492,000 GRT, giving the Carnival Group forty-four ships totalling well over 2 million GRT.

Many of the ships are of the Vista design. Despite being built for different brands, these 85,000-GRT vessels are very similar. Carnival had pioneered the concept of a large series of sister cruise ships. The Vista class (so-called because of the extensive use of glass in the superstructure) is a Panamax-type cruise ship (with a beam capable of transiting the Panama Canal) built by Fincantieri of Italy for Holland America Line, P&O Cruises, Cunard Line and Costa Cruises. The ships are equipped with a diesel-electric power plant and an Azipod propulsion system, and are designed to have 85 per cent of the staterooms enjoying ocean views and 67 per cent of them having balconies.

Carnival has expanded by acquiring traditional brands and keeping them very much as they were. Indeed it is doubtful whether guests actually know that they are on a Carnival-owned vessel.

The cruise industry, like other multi-segment industries, has a number of distinct customer bases. There are cruises for those on a budget, and others that are extremely luxurious, price being the difference. There are also those, such as the main Carnival operation, that are for younger vacationers and others for those of more mature years. By building their own brand and acquiring others, Carnival has been able to achieve hyper-growth in an industry where building times are relatively long and where the capital investment required is huge. Carnival is now firmly ensconced in a number of national markets, with its brands catering to different national groups. The national groups shown below represent the majority of guests:

BRAND	TYPE	MARKET
CARNIVAL	STANDARD	NORTH AMERICA
PRINCESS	STANDARD	NORTH AMERICA
P&O	STANDARD	UNITED KINGDOM
P&O (AUSTRALIA)	STANDARD	AUSTRALASIA
COSTA	STANDARD	ITALY
AIDA	STANDARD	GERMANY
OCEAN VILLAGE	STANDARD	UK (TO BE DISCONTINUED)
IBROJET	STANDARD	SPAIN
CUNARD	PREMIUM	UK/NORTH AMERICA
HOLLAND AMERICA	PREMIUM	NORTH AMERICA
SEABOURN	LUXURY	NORTH AMERICA

Figure 6: Carnival brands

The sleek lines of
Carnival Splendor.

Jubilee, one of the older
Carnival ships at St Thomas.

A builder's model of *Caronia* that graced the foyer of her later namesake, the ex-*Vistafjord*.

Cunard acquired the *Vistafjord* from Norwegian America and later renamed her *Caronia*; she now sails as *Saga Ruby*.

Costa is popular with many Italian Americans and was a major player in the US cruise market for many years, but has become more European-oriented in the years since its acquisition by Carnival.

CUNARD

Cunard, founded by Samuel Cunard from Halifax, Nova Scotia (the family having been forced out of the USA as Loyalists after the War of Independence), was the premier passenger shipping company across the Atlantic, with Cunarders crossing that ocean and breaking records since 1840. Many of the later vessels had undertaken cruises out of US ports, but until the 1950s and 1960s Cunard was predominately a liner company. The *Queen Mary*, *Queen Elizabeth* and the second *Mauretania* were emblematic not only of the company, but also of Great Britain. The *Caronia* of 1949 (already discussed) was designed for both the liner trade and cruising.

However, once the liner trade declined due to the advent of the jet transport aircraft (specifically the Boeing 707 and the Douglas DC10), these large liners proved unsuitable for cruising and were withdrawn. *Mauretania*, built in 1939, went in 1965 with her hull painted green (in a similar manner to *Caronia*) for cruising. *Queen Mary* (now preserved at Long Beach) was withdrawn in 1967, followed by *Queen Elizabeth* in 1968.

The smaller vessels, built in the 1950s for the Canada–UK trade, were successfully converted into cruise ships and had long lives. Two of them, *Carinthia* and *Sylvania*, became Sitmar vessels and joined the Princess fleet as *Fair Princess* and *Dawn Princess* respectively (see earlier). The *Queen Elizabeth 2* (*QE2*), launched in 1967 and entering service in 1969, was designed for both liner and cruising service. Withdrawn in 2009 and currently in a static role in Dubai, she was a great favourite with both UK and North American cruisers.

To gain market share in the fast growing US market, Cunard introduced the purpose-built cruise ships *Cunard Ambassador* and *Cunard Adventurer* for Caribbean cruising in 1971–72. *Cunard Ambassador* suffered a bad fire in 1974 and was sold to become a sheep carrier! *Cunard Adventurer* became the *Sunward II* in 1977, then *Triton* in 1991, and sails today as the *Coral* in the Mediterranean. At just over 14,000 GRT, these vessels were a little small for Cunard and were replaced by the 1974-built *Cunard Countess* and *Cunard Princess*. Of 17,000 GRT, both these vessels lasted in Cunard service well into the 1990s and are still in service with new owners.

Cunard as a company had been acquired by Trafalgar House Investments in 1971, then, in 1983, Trafalgar House purchased Norwegian American Cruises by adding *Vistafjord* and *Sagafjord* to the fleet. Ultimately, *Sagafjord* became the *Saga Rose* of the UK Saga company, specialising in cruise vacations for the over fifties, whilst *Vistafjord*, re-named *Caronia* for a brief time by Cunard, before joining her near sister in the Saga fleet as *Saga Ruby*. *Saga Rose* was withdrawn from service in late 2009.

In 1986, Cunard acquired Sea Goddess Cruises and added the luxury 4,260-GRT, 116-guest mega-yachts, *Sea Goddess 1* and *Sea Goddess 2*, to the fleet. These vessels were mainly intended for the international luxury cruise market. Indeed, Seabourn was marketed through Cunard. *Cunard Princess* was chartered by the United States military in 1990 for a period of six months to act as a floating R&R (rest and relaxation) centre for US personnel involved in the Gulf War that followed Iraq's invasion of Kuwait.

In order to expand its US market operation, Cunard joined with the Effjohn Company to form Cunard Crown Cruises in 1993, and in the following year there was further expansion of the US market when Trafalgar House acquired the Royal Viking Line name together with the 37,845-GRT *Royal Viking Sun* (now HAL's *Prinsendam*), one of the highest rated cruise ships at the time. Kvaerner, a Norwegian group that includes paper, oil and shipbuilding amongst its activities, acquired Trafalgar House, and thus Cunard, in 1996. Two years later, in 1998, Kvaerner sold Cunard to the Carnival group for $500 million. Carnival kept the

Holland America's *Maasdam* in Canadian waters.

Sagafjord left Cunard to become the UK's *Saga Rose*; she was withdrawn in late 2009.

Coral began her cruising career for Cunard as *Cunard Adventurer* in the US market.

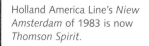

Holland America Line's *Niew Amsterdam* of 1983 is now *Thomson Spirit*.

brand name Cunard, in line with the group's practice of retaining well-known brand names acquired as part of their growth strategy.

At the start of the twenty-first century the Cunard brand itself only offered the *Queen Elizabeth 2* and *Caronia*, with a total of 2,638 berths for the UK/US market on the two ships. However, the *Queen Mary 2* (*QM2*) of 150,000 GRT, (for a period the biggest passenger ship ever built), made her debut in 2003. Carrying a maximum of 2,800 passengers, *QM2* was designed to re-introduce the trans-Atlantic service as well as undertaking cruises from time to time throughout each year. There are also two 85,000-GRT new-builds, *Queen Victoria* (2007) and *Queen Elizabeth* (2010).

Holland America

The Holland America Line (HAL) was founded in 1873 as the Dutch-America Steamship Company, soon becoming known as Holland America. The company's first ships sailed between Rotterdam and New York, (actually the Hoboken Terminal in New Jersey), in 1872. In 1895, the company offered its first cruise, although its second cruise, from the US to the Holy Land, was not undertaken until 1910. In 1971, HAL suspended its trans-Atlantic guest service and became a cruise-only operation.

The company's most famous vessels were both very popular ones in the North American market – *Niew Amsterdam* of 1939, a classic ship that served as a troopship, a trans-Atlantic liner and finally as a cruise ship until 1974, and *Rotterdam* of 1959, that lasted until 1997 when she was sold to Premier Cruise Line. In Premier service, she became *Rembrandt* (also known as *Big Red Boat IV*). Withdrawn in 2000, in 2008 she arrived back in the Netherlands for preservation under her original name.

In 1989, the company became a wholly owned subsidiary of the Carnival Corporation.

As of 2009, HAL operated thirteen vessels ranging from the 38,000-GRT *Prinsendam* through to the 82,000-GRT *Westerdam*. (In October 1980, *Prinsendam* of 1973 caught fire and sank in the Gulf of Alaska whilst re-positioning to the Far East. This could have been a major tragedy, but thanks to the heroics of the crew and the US Coastguard, 324 passengers and 200 crew were rescued in a dramatic operation with no casualties).

Despite ownership by Carnival, HAL ships carry Dutch names and have a European ambience, together with premier service standards.

The Merger of Carnival and P&O Princess

Carnival attempted to acquire other operators, notably Premier Cruises and Royal Caribbean, but without success. In 2002, however, the Carnival Corporation made a counter bid for P&O Princess (i.e. the cruise operation of P&O, not the ferries etc). P&O Princess was on the point of a 51:49 per cent merger with Royal Caribbean, and the offer made by Carnival was difficult for the shareholders to refuse.

With her trademark smokestack changed, Carnival's *Tropicale* became Costa *Tropicale*, but remained within the Carnival Group.

Despite concerns that the various competitor agencies in the US, UK and European Union might veto the deal, it went through. The concept that was adopted in 2003 was for a dual-listed company, whereby Carnival and P&O would retain their identities and brands. As P&O were active in Germany and Australasia, this made the Carnival Corporation truly global. Today, P&O and Princess are separate Carnival Group brands.

Later Carnival Acquisitions and Disposals

In 2007 the latest acquisition was the Spanish operator, Ibrojet. Thus, by 2007 the Carnival Group had a firm footing in the US, UK, Dutch, Australian, German and Spanish cruise markets, and was a true global operator. It did not only operate on a global basis, but served a variety of different national markets. One of the great advantages for the Carnival Group has been in the design of standard new ships (the Vista Class), only making superficial changes to suit the various national markets, and in the ability to switch vessels around within the group in order to respond to market growth.

Thus, *Queen Victoria* being built for Cunard was transferred to P&O as *Arcadia* whilst still on the stocks, and *Pacific Star* of P&O (Australia) had been the *Costa Tropicale*, and initially the *Tropicale* of Carnival Cruises. When the ship was moved from Carnival Cruises to Costa she lost her trademark Carnival winged funnel (smokestack) and received a typical Costa yellow one. The movement of ships within the group has become a feature of the Carnival operation, older vessels being used to strengthen newly acquired brands. In 2007, Carnival sold the Windstar operation to Ambassadors International.

Built as Royal Caribbean's *Song of America*, she became Airtours' *Sunbird* and then *Thomson Destiny*. Here she shares Funchal, Madeira, with a multitude of sailboats.

Still carrying her Viking Lounge on her smokestack, *Long Jie* entered the Asian market in 2007 but came out as *Sun Viking* for Royal Caribbean in 1972.

ROYAL CARIBBEAN

Royal Caribbean Cruise Line was founded in 1968 by Norwegian shipping interests. As discussed earlier, the first ship, *Song of Norway*, entered service two years later. Capacity was doubled the next year with the addition of *Nordic Prince* to the fleet. *Sun Viking* followed in 1972. After four years of successful operation, Royal Caribbean's *Song of Norway* became their first ship to be lengthened, through the insertion of an 85ft midships section. *Nordic Prince* was similarly stretched in 1980. In 1982, Royal Caribbean launched the *Song of America*, over twice the size of *Sun Viking* and, at the time, the third largest cruise ship afloat.

In 1986, Royal Caribbean began the trend of owning 'private Caribbean islands' for North American cruise guests with the purchase of a coastal property – Labadee in Haiti (these properties are not always islands and are only private in the widest use of the word). In 1988, *Sovereign of the Seas*, the largest guest vessel afloat at the time, was launched, and was followed two years later by *Nordic Empress* and *Viking Serenade*. At that time, Royal Caribbean purchased its second private destination, Little Stirrup Cay, an island in the Bahamas, which they re-christened Coco Cay.

Following the introduction of *Song of Norway*, *Nordic Prince* and *Sun Viking*, Royal Caribbean had grown to be number two in the US market. Introduced in 1981, *Song of America*, at over 37,000 GRT, was followed in 1987 by the huge (for the time) 73,192-GRT *Sovereign of the Seas*. With over 2,200 passengers she introduced the suffix '...*of the Seas*' for the company's ships, and the policy of larger and larger vessels. *Monarch of the Seas*, the second ship of the *Sovereign of the Seas* class, entered service the next year, and the third, *Majesty of the Seas*, one year later.

More growth followed. *Nordic Prince* was replaced by the newly built *Legend of the Seas* of the Vision class in 1995 (although *Vision of the Seas* herself did not debut until 1998). Two more Vision-class vessels entered service, *Splendor of the Seas* and *Grandeur of the Seas*, in 1996.

Just as Princess introduced mega and slightly smaller ships in parallel from the late 1980s onwards, so Royal Caribbean introduced a series of classes of differing sizes in an overlapping pattern:

1987–2003 Voyager Class – 5 vessels
132,000 GRT+
3,500+ passengers

2001 – 2003 Radiance Class – 5 vessels
90,000 GRT+
2,200+ passengers

1995 – 1998 Vision Class – 6 vessels
78,000 GRT+
2,000+ passengers

Royal Caribbean introduced rock climbing at sea.

Song of America, now *Thomson Destiny*.

Majesty of the Seas at Key West.

Independence of the Seas was the largest cruise ship ever built, until the debut of *Oasis of the Seas*.

Celebrity Summit anchored off Istanbul's Golden Horn.

Century was a second generation new-build for Celebrity Cruises.

2006 – 2008 Freedom Class – 3 vessels
154,000 GRT+
3,800+ passengers

2009/2010 Project Genesis (*Oasis of the Seas* & *Allure of the Seas*)
220,000 GRT
5,400+ passengers

As the vessels became larger and larger, so more and more facilities are introduced. Ice skating, rock climbing and huge shopping malls became a feature of Royal Caribbean vessels. By 2009, the company was advertising its cruises as the 'Nation of Why Not? Cruising on these mega-ships had gone beyond simply a resort to a whole 'country of cruising'. It sometimes begs the question as to whether it is necessary to ever go ashore – some guests do not. It also brings into question the nomenclature of the customer. Are they still passengers, are they guests, are they cruisers or perhaps – if Royal Caribbean are forecasting the future – citizens?

There has been an ongoing battle between Carnival and Royal Caribbean to have the biggest cruise ship in the world. Carnival introduced the first 100,000-GRT vessel, then Princess went further. Royal Caribbean's Voyager class then tipped the scales at 132,000+ GRT. Then Cunard, now part of Carnival, introduced *Queen Mary 2* at nearly 150,000 GRT so she could claim the title – but not for long. Royal Caribbean introduced *Freedom of the Seas*, 154,000 GRT, giving her the title. Finally, in 2009, the first of Royal Caribbean's Project Genesis vessels, the 220,000 GRT *Oasis of the Seas* entered service. Can cruise ships become larger? Who knows?

Celebrity Cruises/Celebrity Expedition/Azamara Cruises

In 1988, Chandris created a new brand, Celebrity, aimed at North America. The first vessel, *Meridian*, was the refitted *Galileo* (ex-*Galileo Galilei*) of Chandris Cruises. She lasted until 1997, when she became the *Sun Vista* owned by Singapore interests. She sank after a fire in the Far East in 1999, fortunately with no fatalities.

The first new-builds for Celebrity were strikingly modern. *Horizon* (1990) and *Zenith* (1992) were the first new ships ever commissioned by Chandris. At nearly 47,000 GRT, they were followed in 1995, 1996 and 1997 by the 72,000–76,500 GRT *Century*, *Galaxy* and *Mercury* with over 1,800 guests – with an impressive guest/space ratio.

In 2000, the appropriately named *Millennium*, of over 90,000 GRT, was introduced, followed by three sisters, *Constellation*, *Infinity* and *Summit*. These ships were spectacular and clearly aimed at the premium market.

Celebrity then entered the mega-ship era in 2008 with the 117,200-GRT *Celebrity Solstice*, followed by her sisters *Celebrity Equinox* (2009) and *Celebrity Eclipse* (2010). All of the current Celebrity vessels have been re-named by the addition of the prefix Celebrity, e.g. *Celebrity Millennium*, and they are registered in Valetta, Malta, for, amongst other reasons, the fact that Maltese registry (like that of Bermuda, where Princess registers its ships) allows the captain to perform weddings.

In 2004, Celebrity acquired the 2,842-GRT *Sun Bay* and equipped her for just over ninety passengers as the *Celebrity Xpedition*. In this role she provides a means

The outside elevators on *Celebrity Millennium* were revolutionary when she debuted in 2000.

BRAND	TYPE	MARKET
ROYAL CARIBBEAN	STANDARD	NORTH AMERICAN
CELEBRITY	PREMIUM	NORTH AMERICAN
AZAMARA	PREMIUM	NORTH AMERICAN
CELEBRITY EXPEDITION	LUXURY	NORTH AMERICAN
PULLMANTUR	STANDARD	SPAIN
CROISIERES DE FRANCE	STANDARD	FRANCE
ISLAND CRUISES (PART SHARE		UK/PORTUGUESE/
SOLD 2008)	STANDARD	BRAZIL

Figure 7: Royal Caribbean brands

As with the Carnival Group, Royal Caribbean ships are often moved to the new acquisitions from the Royal Caribbean and Celebrity fleets.

NORWEGIAN CRUISE LINE

Until Princess Cruises became part of the Carnival Group, the big four of the North American cruise market were Carnival Group, Royal Caribbean, Princess and Norwegian Cruise Line (NCL).

NCL began operations in 1966 under the name Norwegian Caribbean Line. Recently the company became known for introducing its Freestyle Cruising concept, which means that there are no set times or seating arrangements for meals, nor is formal attire required. Norwegian Cruise Line has a sister company, NCL America, designed to avoid cabotage issues when operating from US ports to Hawaii. NCL itself is jointly owned by Star Cruises of Malaysia and Apollo Management (also owners of Regent Seven Seas and Oceania Cruises), with both companies owning 50 per cent of NCL.

As mentioned, NCL was begun as Norwegian Caribbean Line in 1966 by Knut Kloster and Ted Arison with just one ship, *Sunward*, originally designed for a new cruise-ferry service from Southampton, UK, to Vigo (Spain), Lisbon and Gibraltar. Despite great promise the route was not a success, especially because at the time the UK and Spain were in dispute about the status of Gibraltar. *Sunward* was moved to Miami to be marketed by Arison on Norwegian Caribbean Line's cruises to Nassau. Compared with the older ships that were then offering cruises from Miami to Nassau, she was extremely modern.

A series of similar, but larger, vessels followed: *Skyward* (1968) also built as a ferry, and *Southward* (1971). There was to have been a sister to *Southward*, *Seaward*, but she was sold whilst building to become the *Spirit of London* for P&O (later *Sun Princess*).

Arison soon left (it is rumoured over money), and formed Carnival Cruise Lines, while Kloster acquired additional ships to expand his Caribbean service. NCL was highly innovative and its value-for-money cruises attracted many younger, family-oriented passengers. As the company expanded to other parts of the world,

Pacific Dream was Celebrity Cruises' *Horizon*, before becoming *Island Star* in a joint venture between Royal Caribbean and First Choice in the UK. She now operates for Royal Caribbean's European subsidiary, Pullmantur.

AZAMARA

In 2007 Celebrity launched a new premium brand that appeared to be in direct competition with Oceania Cruises. Both companies used the ex-Renaissance 30,277 GRT-vessels (see later). *R7*, which had been *Delphin Renaissance* and then *Blue Moon* became *Azamara Quest*, whilst *R5* (later *Blue Dream*) became the *Azamara Journey*.

The Royal Caribbean family has included joint ventures in the UK (Island Cruises, now part of TUI) and latterly Pullmantur Cruises in Spain. With the Royal Caribbean, Celebrity and Azamara brands, the group is the number two in the North American market. Like Carnival, but to a lesser extent, Royal Caribbean has also expanded into other markets:

of visiting the Galapagos Islands, made famous by Charles Darwin. Cruise ships are limited in the islands due to the unique and fragile ecosystem, and Celebrity have gained a good market niche using such a luxurious vessel.

Norwegian Star embarks
guests in Los Angeles.

Norwegian Star lit up for a late night
departure from Cabo San Lucas.

Now a gambling ship operating out of Hong Kong, *SuperStar Aquarius* was originally NCL's *Westward*.

including Alaska, Europe, Bermuda, and Hawaii (NCL America was covered earlier in this volume), Norwegian Caribbean became an inappropriate name and so was changed to Norwegian Cruise Line, thus keeping the same initials. Between 1997 and 2001, the company also operated cruises out of Australia under the title of Norwegian Capricorn Line, still keeping the NCL initials.

In 1979 NCL made a surprise purchase of the French Line flagship and pride of France, (at the time the longest ship in the world), the 66,300-GRT *France*. She was renamed *Norway*, and in a conversion costing more than $100 million, rebuilt as a cruise ship. In 1990 she was given extra decks, which increased her tonnage to over 76,000 GRT. *Norway* was significantly larger than any existing cruise ship, especially those owned and operated by NCL. Her size allowed for extra activities on board and increased guest dining options. It also meant that she was unable to berth alongside in most Caribbean ports, and she was equipped with two landing-craft-style tenders to take guests ashore.

The forerunner of today's mega-ships, she suffered a boiler explosion in May 2003 which forced NCL to withdraw her from service. Laid up in Bremerhaven, Germany, until 2005, she was towed to Malaysia where it was intended that she was put to use as an anchored casino or for overnight casino cruises (very popular in the Far East).These plans did not come to fruition and she was sold for scrap, renamed *Blue Lady*, and in 2006 was beached at Alang, India, graveyard of so many great ships, with claims that she contained toxic materials. In September 2007, the Supreme Court of India issued an order permitting her to be broken up at Alang, despite the presence of large amounts of hazardous asbestos remaining on board.

The purchase of *France* was not unique for NCL. In 2003, the company announced the purchase of the American-flagged liners *United States* (the fastest

liner ever built) and *Independence* (see earlier under Hawaiian cruising), for use on the NCL America brand. Although NCL has promised to restore *United States* and re-introduce her to active service, the future of the great ship remains uncertain, and at the time of writing she was still laid up and quite forlorn. It is a sad indictment that the fastest liner ever is being allowed to decay slowly. The sale of *Independence*, renamed *Oceanic*, was noted earlier.

Royal Viking Star and *Royal Viking Sky* were acquired in 1984, and by 1991 had been renamed *Westward* and *Sunward* respectively. NCL also began to build a series of very modern ships, beginning with the *Dreamward* of 1992 (renamed *Norwegian Dream*) and the *Windward* of 1993 (later *Norwegian Wind*), both of over 39,000 GRT. The Baltic ferry, *Viking Saga*, built in 1980, was acquired as the *Leeward* in 1995. In 1996, the third of the Royal Viking trio, *Royal Viking Sea*, became *Norwegian Star*, introducing an era when all their ships would be prefixed by 'Norwegian'.

A series of vessels followed, amongst them *Norwegian Dawn* (2002), *Norwegian Gem* (2007), *Norwegian Jade* (ex-*Pride of Hawaii*), *Norwegian Jewel* (2005), *Norwegian Pearl* (2006) and *Norwegian Star* (2001), all of just over 90,000 GRT. NCL had not opted for mega-ships until 2010, with the introduction of *Norwegian Epic* of 153,000 GRT. This ship and her later sister will bring NCL into the same league as the Carnival Group and Royal Caribbean. In 2009, *Norwegian Dream* and *Norwegian Majesty* left the fleet after their sale to Louis Cruise Lines of Cyprus.

In 1998, NCL acquired a subsidiary, Orient Lines (not to be confused with the British Orient Line company of an earlier era). Orient Lines operated the *Marco Polo* (ex-*Alexander Pushkin*) on a variety of interesting worldwide destinations. Orient Lines ceased to operate in 2008, although a new owner has been rumoured. However, in 2000, NCL itself was acquired by Star Cruises of Malaysia, then in August 2007 Star Cruises sold 50 per cent of NCL for $1 billion to New York-based Apollo Management (owners of Oceania Cruises and Regent Seven Seas Cruises – run as Prestige Cruise Holdings), because NCL's financial position was not as strong as it might have been.

In January 2007, *Norwegian Wind* was transferred to the fleet of Star Cruises, becoming their *SuperStar Aquarius*. Later in the same year, NCL announced that *Pride of Aloha*, one of the two remaining NCL America ships, would be withdrawn from service in May.

Two noteworthy NCL innovations in recent times are the addition of striking hull murals on its vessels and the provision of freestyle cruising. The latter concept is now widely copied, appealing especially to those who wish to have a far more relaxed dining option. Hitherto, most ships operated quite rigid dining arrangements in their main restaurants, with one or two sittings for dinner at allocated tables (exceptions, of course, being specialty and alternative restaurants widely available today). Fixed table arrangements are fine if one's table companions are congenial, but can be difficult if they are not, and on a full ship table changes can be problematic.

CHAPTER EIGHT

The Luxury Market

Whilst cruise vacations are now available to those on more modest incomes, there is still a thriving market, no where more so than in the USA, for high-end luxury cruises. Seabourn, Sea Dream Yacht Club, Oceania Cruises, Regent Seven Seas Cruises, Azamara Cruises, Renaissance Cruises and Silverseas all operate in this sector. Their products offer more spacious accommodation, are often all inclusive, and have higher cuisine and service standards.

SEABOURN CRUISE LINE

Seabourn was founded in 1986 as a subsidiary of the Norwegian cruise ship giant, Kloster Cruise, under the name Signet Cruise Lines, but adopted the name Seabourn Cruise Line shortly afterward. Its first ship, *Seabourn Pride*, entered service in 1988, followed by an identical sister, *Seabourn Spirit*, in 1989. A third vessel, originally planned for 1990, was delayed due to financial constraints at Kloster and was ultimately delivered in 1992 as *Royal Viking Queen* for Royal Viking Line, another Kloster company. In 1994, *Royal Viking Queen* was transferred to another Kloster subsidiary, Royal Cruise Line, as *Queen Odyssey*, before finally joining the Seabourn fleet in 1995 as *Seabourn Legend*.

Following Kloster Cruise's bankruptcy in 1996, Carnival Corporation acquired an interest in Seabourn, and then acquired the remaining shares from NCL in 1998, buying the remaining 50 per cent of Seabourn from NCL Holdings Ltd. The brand was merged into Cunard, and three Cunard ships – *Sea Goddess I*, *Sea Goddess II*, and *Royal Viking Sun* – were transferred into the Seabourn fleet as *Seabourn Goddess I*, *Seabourn Goddess II*, and *Seabourn Sun*.

In 2001, *Seabourn Goddess I* and *Seabourn Goddess II* were sold to Sea Dream Yacht Club, and then in 2002, *Seabourn Sun* was transferred to the Carnival-owned Holland America Line as the *Prinsendam*, reducing the Seabourn fleet to its three original sister ships, although a new vessel is planned.

SEA GODDESS/SEA DREAM YACHT CLUB

Sea Goddess I and *Sea Goddess II* were built in 1984 and 1985 by Wärtsilä, Helsinki, for Sea Goddess Cruises of Norway. After a poor season in 1986, they were chartered to Cunard for twelve years. Cunard continued to market them as *Sea Goddess I* and *Sea Goddess II*. Following the acquisition of Cunard by Carnival in 1998, the ships were transferred to Carnival's Seabourn operation and renamed *Seabourn Goddess I* and *Seabourn Goddess II*. In 2001, they were sold to new company SeaDream Yacht Club, owned by Atle Brynstead, founder of Seabourn, and renamed *Sea Dream I* and *Sea Dream II*.

THE RENAISSANCE EXPERIMENT

Renaissance began operations with eight similar small luxury cruise ships between 1989 and 1992. The first four, Renaissance I–IV, carried 100 guests in fifty cabins with seventy-two crew. The second four carried 114 guests in fifty-seven cabins with seventy-two crew.

Between 1998 and 2002 Renaissance commissioned 8 sisters, R1–R8. 30,277 GRT, with accommodation for around 700. These ships were very elegant and offered four evening dining options, which allowed for plenty of choice.

On the collapse of Renaissance on 25 September 2001, six of the sisters (all except *R3* and *R4* in the Pacific) were moved to Gibraltar, where they were temporarily laid up pending disposal. Extremely popular ships, all eight are now in service with other companies.

Oceania Cruises has:
R1 as *Insignia*
R2 as *Regatta*
R5 as *Nautica* (ex-*Blue Dream*)

Not all Miami terminals are all hustle and bustle: Oceania's *Regatta* bunkers amid the calm at Terminal J.

Seabourn Pride moored in Venice.

Sea Dream 1 – almost a private yacht.

Royal Princess, ex-*R8*, ex-*Minerva 2* will re-enter the UK market as *Adonia* in May 2011.

Princess has:

R8 as *Royal Princess* (ex-*Minerva 2*)

R4 as *Ocean Princess* (ex-*Tahitian Princess*)

R3 as *Pacific Princess*

Azamara Cruises has:

R6 as *Azamara Journey* (ex-*Blue Star*, ex-*Blue Dream*)

R7 as *Azamara Quest* (ex-*Blue Moon*, ex-*Delphin Renaissance*)

With eight quite beautiful and well-equipped mid-sized ships, why did Renaissance fail? The tragedy of 9/11 played a major role, as the company was very dependent on fly cruising, and the reluctance to fly on the part of US guests in the aftermath of the terrorist attacks on New York and Washington DC proved to be the final nail in the coffin: the company declared bankruptcy soon afterwards on 25 September 2001.

However, it is now widely believed that the company had a flawed marketing strategy, for they sold direct to the customer and did not use the services of travel agents. Towards the end, the company did begin to rebuild relationships with travel agents, but it was too late. Once problems began, passengers found that they had no agents to rely on to get them home again. Renaissance was also criticised for a heavy advance payment schedule, which had caused some travel insurers to cease covering their cruises. Despite the failure of the company, the beauty and quality of their virtually new R-class ships was almost legendary – evidenced by the speed at which they were snapped up by other operators following Renaissance's demise.

CRYSTAL CRUISES

Perhaps not a name that is readily recognised outside the shipping industry, Nippon Yusen Kaisha (NYK) is in fact the largest shipping company in the world, operating over 800 ships. In its home country of Japan, the company operates Asuka Cruises. In 1988, the company formed Crystal Cruises as a luxury brand, primarily aimed at the North American market. The first ship, *Crystal Harmony* (launched in 1990), 51,042 GRT and carrying a maximum 1,010 guests, became *Asuka 2* in 2005, leaving the 51,044-GRT, 940-guest *Crystal Symphony* of 1995 and the 68,870-GRT, 1,080-guest *Crystal Serenity* of 2003, to operate the Crystal Cruise package.

Crystal has developed a loyal following and a reputation for luxury and quality. Amongst the many awards that Crystal has received, the company was voted the 'World's Best Large-Ship Cruise Line' in *Travel & Leisure* magazine's annual readers' survey in 2006 for an eleventh consecutive year. The company is the only cruise line, resort or hotel to have won the prestigious award each year since the award's inception.

In late 2006, *Crystal Symphony* underwent a major refit at BAE Systems in Norfolk, VA, when the $23 million spend resulted in a vessel that was virtually new internally.

Crystal Symphony berthed in Amsterdam.

Silver Cloud in the Mediterranean.

Silver Whisper in calm seas.

Seven Seas' *Mariner*
in Thai waters.

Regatta, the first
Oceania vessel
was built as *R2*.

One of the beautiful R ships
of Renaissance Cruise, *R5* now
sails as Oceania's *Nautica*.

Oceania's *Insignia* (built as
R1) on a cold New Year's
Day in a Chilean fjord.

SILVERSEAS CRUISES

The company has its origins in the Sitmar Line (Societa Italiana Transporti Marittimi), originally founded in 1954 in Genoa. Sitmar was purchased by P&O, as described earlier, but some off those associated with Sitmar decided in the early 1990s to enter a new area, the luxury end of the cruise business. There was, at the time, a gap in the market between small ships, such as those operated by Cunard (*Sea Goddess 1 & 2*) *Seabourn Legend, Sprit & Pride*, and Radisson's *Song of Flower* (ex-*Explorer Starship*, ex-*Begonia*), and the larger vessels such as the 37,845-GRT *Royal Viking Sun*, with accommodation for up to 814.

The newly formed Silversea Cruises commissioned two sister ships, *Silver Cloud* and *Silver Wind*, each of 16,800 GRT with a capacity of 296, to enter service in 1994. As a comparison, NCL's *Southward*, of very similar tonnage, has a capacity in excess of 900: Silverseas guests have three times more room giving a guest/space ratio of 56.8 compared with *Southward's* 17.

The vessels were built by the Francesco Visentini yard in Donada, Italy, and fitted out by Mariotti in Genoa. The design team were Petter Yran and Bjorn Storbratten and cost in excess of $300 million each. *Silver Wind* was delivered in 1994, with *Silver Cloud* following in 1995. In 1998, Silverseas announced that they had ordered two new vessels for delivery in 2000 and 2001; *Silver Shadow* and *Silver Whisper*. Then, in January 2010, the 36,000-GRT *Silver Spirit* was introduced with a guest capacity of 540.

In 1997, Silverseas began a partnership with the *National Geographic Traveler* series, and there were eight National Geographic cruises in 1998. The success of these voyages led to the acquisition, in 2008, of *Prince Albert II* (ex-*Delphin Clipper*, ex-*World Adventure*, ex-*Delphin Clipper*, ex-*Delphin Star*, ex-*Sally Clipper*, ex-*Baltic Clipper*, ex-*Dream 21*, ex-*World Discover*). Refitted, the vessel, built in 1989, carries around 132 guests on luxurious expedition-style destination cruises. Designed specifically for navigating remote areas, including both polar regions, the 6,072-ton vessel boasts a strengthened hull with the highest Lloyd's Register ice-class notation (1A) for passenger ships.

REGENT SEVEN SEAS

Seven Seas Cruise Line was founded by the Kawasaki Kisen Kaisha Line and Skaugen. Radisson Diamond Cruises took over Seven Seas Cruises in 1995, with its ship *Song of Flower*, and the combined company became Radisson Seven Seas Cruises: today, it is known as Regent Seven Seas Cruises.

Song of Flower was built as the freighter *Begonia* in 1974 for Fearnley & Eger. In 1985, she was rebuilt in Bremerhaven as the exploration cruise ship *Explorer Starship*. She was chartered to Exploration Cruise Line until their bankruptcy in 1988. Fearnley & Eger reacquired the ship in February 1993, following her

conversion into a luxury cruise ship, and renamed her *Song of Flower*. In 2003, the ship was sold again, this time to Cie des Iles du Ponant.

Regent's vessels are mid-sized and operate at the premium end of the market. From 1992 until 2005, the company operated the *Radisson Diamond* – an 18,600-GRT catamaran with accommodation for 354 guests. As her machinery was well away from any guest areas, she was very quiet. She now operates as a gambling ship, the *Asia Star*, out of Hong Kong.

Regent is renowned for its cuisine and service. Apollo Management, the investment group, purchased the company from Carlson Companies for $1 billion, with the deal concluded in February 2008. Apollo, through Prestige Cruise Holdings, also owns Oceania Cruises and 50 per cent of Norwegian Cruise Line. By the end of 2009, the Regent brand was operating 41,500-GRT *Seven Seas Voyager* (45,000 GRT – 2003), *Seven Seas Mariner* (48,000 GRT – 2001) and *Seven Seas Navigator* (28,500 GRT – 1999). The company also operated *Paul Gauguin* in the Pacific from 2005 until 2010 on behalf of her owners.

OCEANIA CRUISES

The demise of Renaissance Cruises in September 2001 brought the eight Renaissance R ships, each of 30,277 GRT and accommodating up to 684 guests, onto the market. In 2002, Frank Del Rio, a senior executive and CEO of Renaissance Cruises, and Joseph Watters, who had held the position of President of Crystal Cruises and prior to that, President of Royal Viking Line and President of Princess Cruises, formed a new company, Oceania Cruises.

Initially chartering one ship, *Regatta* (ex-*R2*) the company began to build a loyal following, with its informal luxury based on a country house-style operation. *Regatta* made her debut for the company on 5 July 2003. The success of the operation led to rapid expansion with *Insignia* (ex-*R1*) chartered in 2004, and *Nautica* (ex-*R5*) following in 2005.

By 2007 the company was operating on a global basis, and attracting not just North American but an increasing number of UK and other nationalities, inheriting many of the loyal Renaissance Cruises guests. The company had wanted to acquire one or more of the remaining R ships, but this was not possible.

In 2007, the company was acquired by Apollo Management, a New York private equity company, for $850 million. Leaving the Oceania management team intact, the new owners announced a major expansion programme. Firstly the *Regatta*, *Nautica* and *Insignia* were purchased from the charterers, and it was announced that orders had been placed for two 65,000-GRT ships from the Genoa yard of Fincantieri. These are scheduled for delivery in 2010 and 2011, and there is an option of a third vessel for delivery in 2012. The new ships will accommodate up to 1,260 guests and have been designed by Yran & Storbratten.

CHAPTER NINE

Niche Markets

Not all cruises are of a traditional nature, and these days there are a number of niches that often appeal to those who want to take their cruising to a different level or style.

ADVENTURE CRUISING

Adventure cruising to the Antarctic, or sail cruising around the Caribbean, tend to attract a more international clientele. One form of niche cruising that can be considered to belong to the North American market is in the form of the small ships that ply up both the east and west coasts of the USA, carrying a small number of passengers.

Cruise West operate a series of ships, all named 'Spirit of...', that operate eco-tours. The Antarctic, protected by international agreements, is a rapid growth area for cruising. Mainstream cruise ships out of Ushuaia give guests a close-up look at the 'white continent', even if landing (and shopping!) options are limited. There will need to be great care taken to ensure that cruising does not damage the already fragile environment.

The loss of *Explorer* in 2007, operated by the Canadian firm GAP Adventures, after the ship was holed by ice, does not appear to have dampened enthusiasm for cruising in the Antarctic region. More than 150 passengers and crew (ninety-one passengers, nine expedition staff, fifty-four crew) were safely evacuated near the South Shetland Islands, 120km north of the Antarctic peninsula. After 4 or 5 hours in open lifeboats in active seas, guests were transferred from lifeboats to Hurtigruten's *Nordnorge* which was in the area.

SAILING SHIP CRUISES

Perhaps there is something in the human psyche that harks back to days of yore. Sailing ships as major carriers of goods gave way to steam, and then diesel power, in the first half of the twentieth century, but the sailing cruise ship is a recent phenomenon that has been gaining a loyal following.

Sea Cloud, of Sea Cloud Cruises, was built in Germany in the 1930s as the largest sailing yacht in the world. Originally named *Hussar*, she was ordered by E. F. Hutton for his wife, Marjorie Merryweather. After their divorce his wife gained the vessel, which she renamed *Sea Cloud*. The ship served the US Coastguard during the Second World War, before becoming the Dominican Republic's presidential yacht. After a major refit in 1979, she regained her *Sea Cloud* name and entered service as a cruise ship, catering for sixty-four guests. In 2000, she was joined by a new-build, Sea *Cloud 2*, designed for ninety-four guests, and a third vessel is currently on order.

Bareboat charters of small sailing craft have been a regular feature of the Caribbean and the Aegean for some years, but in 1990 Club Mediterranee introduced *Club Med 1* (now *Wind Surf* of Windstar Cruises), followed by *Club Med 2* in 1992. Carrying over 300 guests, these vessels brought luxury to sailing ship cruising and provided an opportunity for more and more vacationers to enjoy this type of cruise. Today, Windstar Cruises operate a fleet of three luxury hi-tech sailing vessels with computer controlled sails. Their appearance is very different from the classic perception of a sailing ship.

More traditional, but still in the premium market, are the vessels of Star Clipper Cruises. *Star Clipper* and *Star Flyer* of the early 1990s, designed for 170 guests, were joined in 2000 by the mighty *Royal Clipper*. Carrying 227 guests, she was inspired by the German vessel, *Preussen*, of 1902, and remains the only five-masted sailing vessel built since then. Complete with a lounge below the waterline where guests can view marine life face to face, she is a truly magnificent and luxurious vessel. The majority of passengers on these vessels will be from North America.

Bareboat cruises, such as those offered by Windjammer, have guests performing many of the duties of the crew, and are more akin to a private charter. But at whatever level, sailing cruise vessels allow passengers to relive the great days of sail in comfort and luxury – albeit at a premium price befitting an exclusive product.

Built by E.F. Hutton for his wife, *Sea Cloud* is now an extremely graceful cruise vessel.

A luxury alternative – *Star Flyer* at St Kitts.

River Cruises

Europe has long been known for its river cruising, with the Rhine being a particular favourite. Today the Seine, the Danube, the Volga, the route between Moscow and St Petersburg are just a few of the European river cruise destinations targeted at an international market. The Far East has also developed river cruising. One of the earliest purpose-built cruise ships was the small *North American* of 1913. She had a long life on the Great Lakes, sinking under tow in 1967. Her wreck was discovered in 2006.

In the US, the prime river cruise venue has been the Mississippi, and the vessel best associated with this river is the *Delta Queen*, the only moving US National Historic Landmark. *Delta Queen* is a traditional sternwheel steamboat. Up to the Second World War, the vessel provided a regular service up and down the Mississippi, until the development of roads rendered the service un-economic. Three different US Presidents have sailed on *Delta Queen*: Herbert Hoover, Harry Truman and Jimmy Carter.

In 1946, *Delta Queen* was purchased by Greene Line Steamers, and ownership of the vessel has changed a number of times since 1971. *Delta Queen* operates with a presidential exemption to the law prohibiting the operation of overnight guest vessels with wooden superstructures. Her Betty Blake Lounge is named in honour of the lady who rose from secretary to president of the steamship line, and who lobbied for the exemption. In 2008, Majestic Cruise Lines withdrew the vessel from service citing safety reasons, resulting in an outcry. Nonetheless, since June 2009 she has been docked in Chattanooga, Tennessee, where she has been converted into a hotel.

Delta Queen was listed on the National Register of Historic Places in 1970, and was further declared a National Historic Landmark in 1989. Currently there are no cruises operating on the river, but hopefully this will change. Majestic's other vessels, *America Queen* and *Mississippi Queen*, await buyers, as do their west coast vessels.

Windsurf departing Messina.

FREIGHTER CRUISES

There are fewer and fewer options today for cruising on a freighter. Containerisation has led to the demise of the standard break-bulk cargo ship, many of which carried a small number of passengers. Nevertheless, if one is prepared for long periods at sea and docking in out of the way ports with only the company of a very few fellow passengers, freighter cruising is still possible. A useful website is www.freightercruises.com.

WORLD CRUISES

World cruises started to gain popularity after the First World War. Cunard and Canadian Pacific offered world cruises to a mainly rich US, Canadian, British and European clientele. Later, P&O joined the round-the-world cruise market, and after the Second World War American President Lines became renowned for its 100-day cruises around the world from Jersey City, with the fare a mere $30 per diem in 1963.

In the 1960s, Holland America, using *Rotterdam*, and Royal Rotterdam Lloyd, using *Willem Ruys* (later to become the ill-fated *Achille Lauro*), began to offer world cruises out of the US.

For those who can spare between ninety and 110 days, a world cruise can be a once in a lifetime experience, taking in many different cultures. Although having said that, some people take one regularly!

In 2010, the opportunities for American market world cruising were greater than ever. Holland America, Regent Seven Seas Cruises, Cunard, Silverseas, Crystal and Seabourn were all offering world cruises out of US ports. In addition, P&O, Saga and Fred Olsen offered world cruises out of the UK, with Princess starting a world cruise in Sydney, Australia. Perhaps the ultimate is the 300+-day world cruise out of Singapore, operated by Cruise West on *Spirit of Oceanus*.

DAY & GAMBLING CRUISING

For those who cannot afford the time or money for even a mini-cruise, Florida offers the opportunity for day cruises, which are more often than not linked to gambling. There are small gambling boats operating out of ports such as Jacksonville and other Florida ports. For example, Oceans 21 operate gambling cruises on their *Casino Royale*, and *Ocean Jewel of St Petersburg* out of Tampa and St Petersburg, whilst the *Palm Beach Princess* (ex-*Viking Princess*) fulfils the same role for the palm Beach Casino Line out of Palm Beach, Florida.

On a larger scale, Island Cruises offer day trips to Grand Bahama Island out of Fort Lauderdale, as does the Discovery Cruise Line. For many years Discovery Cruise Line operated an ex-North Sea and a Canary Islands–UK ferry *Discovery* (ex-*Blenheim*, not to be confused with the *Discovery*, ex-*Island Princess* of

UK-based Voyages of Discovery). Currently the company has been using the *Discovery Sun* (ex-*Freeport*, ex-*Scandinavian Star*) which was originally built as a Baltic ferry. There are also gambling ships operating out of Gary, Indiana (*Majestic Star*) and other US ports in states where gambling is not permitted onshore.

RESIDENTIAL CRUISE SHIPS

It has long been a joke amongst regular cruise-ship passengers that it might be cheaper to live on a ship after retirement than in residential care. The figures actually support this idea, and there have been instances of people living more or less full time on cruise ships.

The concept of a ship of luxury apartments was realised with the introduction of *The World* by Residensea in 2002. Originally, Knut Kloster Jr had planned for a ship of twice *The World*'s 43,000 GRT, which offers 165 apartments ranging from 1 to 3 bedrooms. In recent years she has operated more like a conventional – rather than a residential – cruise ship. Whilst there are plans for further residential ships, these are at an early stage. Perhaps the most ambitious is for the *Supership Freedom* – 4,320ft, 2.7 million GRT, 50,000 guests with 15,000 crew and its own airfield!

A Clyde Mallory liner which offered coastal cruises between Floriada and New York. (Courtesy Dover Publications)

The *World of Residensea*
at Inchon.

Matson Line's beautiful *Lurline*. (Courtesy Dover Publications)

Matson Line's *Matsonia*. (Courtesy Dover Publications)

THE NEW S.S. *Independence* and S.S. *Constitution*

The classic lines of *Independence* and *Constitution*. (Courtesy Dover Publications)

Moore–McCormack's *Brazil* offered line voyages and cruises between South America and the US. (Courtesy Dover Publications)

Line voyages also become cruises, a Panama Pacific liner in the Panama Canal. (Courtesy Dover Publications)

Peninsular & Occidental's *Cuba* departs Havana.

CHAPTER TEN

The Future and Market Vulnerability

By 2007, with predictions of 12 million Americans cruising by 2010, the market seems to be both secure and growing. However, the global financial crisis of 2008–9 and perhaps onwards has brought new challenges to the global cruise industry and, as the largest segment, the American cruise market cannot avoid these issues. Certain trends can be discerned:

Since 9/11 there has been a growth in the use of US base ports to reduce overseas flights. New terminals are springing up as municipalities see the possibilities of attracting more and more revenue from both cruise companies and their guests. However, North Americans seem more willing to travel again and the range of far-flung destinations is increasing.

The number of companies is decreasing through take overs and mergers. This is a normal business cycle. New companies start up and either fail or, if successful, become prey to the larger operators. One UK commentator wondered whether one day quite soon we will stop talking about taking a cruise and replace it with 'taking a Carnival!'

The market is differentiating into mega-ships and smaller, more intimate, ships, with the likelihood of fewer vessels in the intermediate range. The success of companies such as Oceania and Regent Seven Seas has shown that there is a market for the more traditional luxury cruising. On the other hand, the *Oasis of the Seas* class of Royal Caribbean shows how resort ships are likely to develop.

The mega-ships will become bigger and bigger, with more and more facilities. It is worth considering that *Norway*, at 76,000 GRT, was considered huge for a cruise ship in 1979. By 2010, the 220,000 GRT of the *Oasis of the Seas* is likely to be the standard by which size will be measured in the future. The larger the vessel, the more facilities. Royal Caribbean began by advertising floating resorts, but by 2009 it was 'The Nation of Why Not'. Mega-ships are becoming as sophisticated as any vacation resort.

The Caribbean is approaching saturation point for the number of cruise guests it can accommodate. The Far East, Australasia, South America and even the edges of Antarctica will see increasing volumes of North American market cruise ships.

There will be more and more family-oriented cruises and, conversely, more and more cruises for the older generation in child-free ships. The trend has been set by the UK Saga company, with its product specifically aimed at the over fifties. (Saga – Send A Granny Away – as some wag has put it).

Serenade of the Seas
enters Vancouver.

Conclusion

This book has tried to provide a brief overview of the North American cruise market. The full story would take volumes, but hopefully what is provided here will have given an insight into the largest – and still the fastest growing – sector of what must surely be the most exciting, dynamic, and even glamorous vacation business in the whole wide world.

Ambassador II, built as the ferry *Prinz Oberon* for Northern European operations on a short cruise out of Florida for Sterling Casino Lines.

Holland America's *Amsterdam* cruising in Glacier Bay.

Further Reading

Cartwright, R. & Harvey, C., *Cruise Britannia: The History of the British Cruise Ship*, The History Press

Cartwright, R. & Baird, C. *The Development and Growth of the Cruise Industry*, Butterworth–Heinemann

Cartwright, R., *P&O Princess: The Cruise Ships*, The History Press

Cooke, A., *Liners and Cruise Ships: Some Notable Smaller Vessels*, vol.1, Carmania Press

Cooke, A., *Liners and Cruise Ships: Some More Notable Smaller Vessels*, vol.2, Carmania Press

Cooke, A., *Liners and Cruise Ships: Further Notable Smaller Vessels*, vol.3, Carmania Press

Dawson, Philip S., *Cruise Ships: An Evolution in Design*, Conway Maritime Press Ltd

Dickinson, B. & Vladimir, A., *Selling the Sea: An Inside Look at the Cruise Industry*, John Wiley & Sons

Elisio, M., *The Sitmar Liners & The V Ships*, Carmania Press

Fox, R., *Liners: The Golden Age*, Könemann

Garin, Kristopher A., *Devils on the Deep Blue Sea: The Dreams, Schemes, and Showdowns That Built America's Cruise-Ship Empires*, Plume Books

Maxtone-Graham, J., *Crossing and Cruising: Passenger Ships Then and Now, from Ocean Liners Normandie and Aquatania to Cruise Ships Sovereign of the Seas and Seabourn Pride*, Scribers

Maxtone-Graham, J., *Liners to the Sun*, Macmillan

Miller, William H., *The First Great Ocean Liners in Photographs, 1897–1927*, Dover Publications Inc.

Miller, William H., *Great Cruise Ships and Ocean Liners From 1954–1986*, Dover Publications Inc.

Miller, William H., *The Great Luxury Liners, 1927–1954*, Dover Publications Inc.

Miller, William H., *Modern Cruise Ships, 1965–1990*, Dover Publications Inc.

Miller, William H., *Ocean Liner Chronicles*, Carmania Press

Miller, William H., *Pictorial Encyclopaedia of Ocean Liners, 1860–1993*, Dover Publications Inc.

Quartermaine, P. & Peter, B., *Cruise: Identity, Design & Culture*, Laurence King